WHAT'S WRONG WITH MY IGUANA?

John Rossi M.A., D.V.M.

The Herpetocultural Library®

Advanced
Vivarium
Systems, inc.

Copyright©1998 by **ADVANCED VIVARIUM SYSTEMS, INC.**
All Rights Reserved.

Library of Congress Catalog Card Number: 96-183295

ISBN: 1-882770-43-9

PRINTED AND BOUND IN SINGAPORE.

Cover: Green iguana (*Iguana iguana.*)
Photo by David Northcott.

ACKNOWLEDGMENTS

The author would like to express his deepest gratitude to many friends and colleagues who have taught me so much about iguanas over the years. These include some of North America's finest reptile veterinarians, including Steve Barten, Tom Boyer, Richard Funk, the late James Corcoran, Fredric Frye, Elliot Jacobson, Roger Klingenberg, and Doug Mader. I would also like to thank all of my clients who patiently allowed me to photograph their pets and learn from their illnesses. Lastly, I would like to thank my loving wife Roxanne, who has encouraged, supported and participated in my reptile-related activities from the beginning.

DEDICATION

This book is dedicated to my good friend and longtime iguana client, Vic Morgan, who called me at 4:30 in the morning to announce that he had just become the proud grandfather of baby iguanas. No one seemed to understand iguanas better that Vic, who studied their behavior intensively, and repeatedly bred them in captivity. Vic often called me for much needed medical advice, but always taught me something about iguana behavior in return, something I couldn't learn in a book.

WHAT'S WRONG WITH MY IGUANA
John Rossi M.A., D.V.M.

Contents

Introduction...1
Brief Summary of Care in Captivity 2
Handling of Iguanas for Examination and Treatment 4
Performing a Physical Exam 6

SPECIFIC PROBLEMS

Appetite Loss (Anorexia) 8
Bite Wounds 9
Bleeding 10
Broken Tail..11
Burns 12
Cold Exposure..13
Color Change...14
Constipation 15
Dehydration...16
Dental Disease and Stomatitis (Mouth Rot) 17
Dermatitis (Skin Infection) 19
Diarrhea 20
Drowning 22
Dystocia (Egg Binding) 23
Eye Problems...26
Facial (Rostral) Abrasions..27
Failure to Grow 29
Fractures 30
Head Tilt, Circling and Loss of Balance...32
Lameness (Limping)...33
Lumps and Bumps 34
Nail Trimming and Torn Nails..35
Overheating 36
Paralysis and Paresis (Weakness) 37
Parasites (Worms, Mites, Protozoans, and Harmful Bacteria)..........38
Protrusions, Front and Back 40
Respiratory Problems 42
Scoliosis (Curvature of the Spine) 43
Seizures, Tremors and Generalized Weakness 44
Soft Bendable Bones 45

Swelling (Jaws, Abdomen, Toes, Legs, Skin, Eyes and Tail) 46
Trauma 49
Vomiting 50
Problem/Solution Chart..55

SPECIAL TOPICS

Behavior...51
First Aid 54
Gout and Calcification of Soft Tissue 57
Medicines and Medicating 59
Medicines 61
Most Commonly Used Drugs in Iguanas 62
Iguana Antibiotic Chart I...63
Iguana Antibiotic Chart II 64
Metabolic Bone Disease-The Hard Facts..65
Personal Hygiene and Quarantine 67
Preventive Medicine..68
Spaying and Neutering..71
Transportation 72
Veterinarians - Why You Need One and How To Choose One 73
References and Recommended Readings 74

INTRODUCTION

Iguanas are now the most popular reptilian pet in the world. Many books have been written about their care and breeding. Yet, to this date, very few books have been written for the average iguana owner about the common medical problems and first aid of these interesting and complex animals. In fact, this book could have been titled, *THE IGUANA OWNER'S HOME VETERINARY MANUAL*. It is not meant to take the place of a skilled reptile veterinarian. However, it presents in a very organized manner, some of the most common problems that owners of iguanas deal with. Common home treatments and simple veterinary problems and procedures are described.

Problems are presented in alphabetical order in order to simplify their location for quick reference. The book is also very well illustrated, which makes recognition of many problems even easier. The book also has a number of pertinent discussions on special topics, including first aid, medicines and medicating, preventive medicine, spaying and neutering, transportation of iguanas, and how to choose a veterinarian.

So here, in a single, relatively inexpensive book, is an indispensable guide to recognizing your iguana's problems, along with advice on what he or she will need to recover, written by one of the most experienced reptile veterinarians in the country. It will become a valuable addition to your pet library, whether you are an iguana breeder or just own one iguana. In fact, if your veterinarian does not have too much experience with iguanas, he or she may find it helpful as well. Take it with you when you bring in your iguana.

BRIEF SUMMARY OF CARE IN CAPTIVITY

Diet and other aspects of captive care are not discussed in detail in this book. The reader is referred to the **Green Iguana Manual** for all of the details necessary to successfully maintain iguanas. However, there are two main aspects of captive maintenance, namely essential dietary requirements and lighting which will be briefly discussed here in order to help avoid serious medical problems and assist in treating them once they occur.

Briefly, the diet should consist largely of green, leafy vegetables (over 50%) with other vegetables making up most of the rest of the diet. This simple guideline would save more iguanas lives than anything else in this book, if people would just follow it. Specifically, green leafy vegetables such as collard greens, mustard greens, turnip greens or kale are needed almost daily in order to avoid problems in growing or gravid iguanas. If these leafy greens or other similar greens are a larger part of a prepared diet, then that diet will probably also perform well. Fruit should be kept to a minimum for several reasons. Lastly, I do not recommend any animal protein in the diet.

With regard to lighting, some ultraviolet light appears to be a necessity for these lizards. If they receive no UV light, specifically UVB light, they can not manufacture Vitamin D in the skin. Therefore, they can not absorb or utilize calcium, and will start showing some or all of the signs associated with a calcium deficiency. Sources of UVB light include a number of artificial lights and natural unfiltered sunlight. Lights which produce UVB include the following: 1) full spectrum fluorescent such as Vitalites® 2) high UVB reptile bulbs and 3) BL type fluorescent blacklights. They should not be blocked by glass or plexiglass, and should be kept relatively close to the basking area (i.e. no more than 18 inches away). They should be replaced often. I usually recommend intervals of no longer than 6 months for the Vitalites® manufactured at the time of this writing. Remember however, there is no substitute for natural unfiltered sunlight. Artificial lights are not as good as natural sunlight and ultimately iguanas deprived of any natural light will begin to decline in health. So get those iguanas outside as often as you can, even if it is only during the summer. Indeed, even one or two hours of natural light per day may have tremendous long-term benefits. All of the iguanas I have seen that have reached ten years of age or more have had access to natural sunlight for at least part of the year.

With the appropriate diet and lighting, most iguanas will grow and thrive. See the many books on iguana care for more details on husbandry, especially the *Green Iguana Manual* by Philippe de Vosjoli.

Iguanas are large, impressive, long-lived and complicated animals. Preventive maintenance, a little knowledge about first aid, and an experienced reptile veterinarian will help them live a long, healthy life.

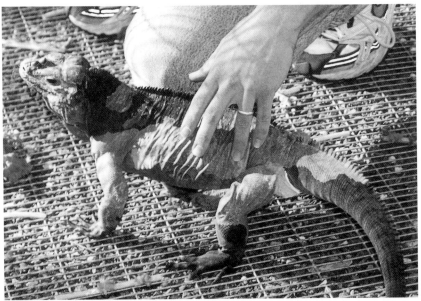

Rhinoceros iguanas (*Cyclura cornuta*) have generally similar requirements as green iguanas and the medical information presented in this book will also apply.

HANDLING OF IGUANAS FOR EXAMINATION AND TREATMENT

Handling iguanas for examination or treatment is different from handling for pleasure. Handling for pleasure usually involves no restraint and the lizard is allowed to crawl over the hands, shoulder or head of the keeper. Restraint involves grasping the lizard firmly behind the head, and then controlling the pelvis and tail. Typically, I grasp the lizard and place the tail in my armpit, thereby controlling the tail to avoid getting whipped. **A large, thick towel is invaluable when dealing with an upset iguana, as it seems to calm the lizard and protect the handler from those razor sharp teeth and claws.** While total restraint is not a pleasurable experience for the iguana, it is necessary in order to conduct a thorough physical exam on most lizards. I always advise my technicians that iguanas must be treated like cats, with either very light restraint or total restraint, and nothing in between. **MAKE NO MISTAKE. MID-SIZED OR LARGER IGUANAS ARE DANGEROUS ANIMALS CAPABLE OF REMOVING YOUR FINGERTIPS. They need to be treated with respect.** Once the decision has been made to restrain, you must restrain them completely. And you must not loosen up during the course of the exam, or they will feel it and bolt forward when you least expect it. **Some individuals are so large and powerful (or aggressive) that chemical restraint is necessary in order to perform a complete physical exam or collect blood for testing.** A drug named Telazol® is ideal for this purpose. I usually use a dose of 4-5 mg/kg intramuscularly to relax a lizard enough to collect blood or perform a physical.

FORCEFUL RESTRAINT IS NOT WITHOUT SOME RISK. Struggling iguanas can injure themselves, especially if they have softer bones than usual. Occasionally, struggling iguanas will rupture blood vessels around their eyes, resulting in a temporarily "pop-eyed" appearance. Of course, these kinds of things should be avoided, and every effort including chemical restraint should be made in order to prevent this kind of trauma.

Sometimes the vasovagal response can be used to help quiet an iguana. This involves applying gentle pressure to both eyes for about thirty seconds. Generally, if performed in a quiet room, most iguanas will relax temporarily and can be closely examined. Be aware that loud noises and touching will rapidly bring the iguana out of its "trance". Placing a soft, self-clinging wrap such as Vet-Wrap® completely around the head is also a useful trick to temporarily calm and restrain a nervous iguana.

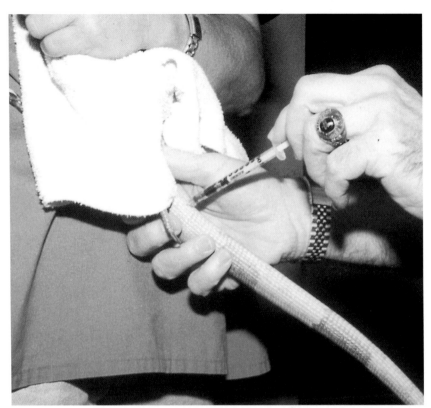

This green iguana is restrained using a towel while a blood sample is obtained.

Remember that restraint is only necessary for a thorough examination or treatment, and if neither is needed, then neither is restraint. Things such as the administration of antibiotics, fluids, or topical medications, as well as bandages, all require restraint. Consult your veterinarian, if you cannot treat as needed.

While restraint does temporarily reduce the iguana's trust of the owner, it re-establishes the dominance of the owner in many cases, and surprisingly, does not seem to cause permanent damage to the iguana-owner relationship.

PERFORMING A PHYSICAL EXAM

Although best performed by a veterinarian, an owner should examine his iguana regularly in order to spot signs of disease early. A physical should be performed in a systematic manner beginning at the front end and working backwards. Before picking the lizard up, look at the demeanor and stance of the animal. Is it alert and supporting itself properly? A "zoned out" or depressed appearance could signal a serious problem; and so could an unusual color. Look at this before you begin to disturb the animal.

Look at the nose (rostral area) first. Is it normal in scalation and color, or is it raw and abraded? Is it swollen and puffy or smooth and firmly attached to the underlying bone? If not, you may have a problem such as an abscess. *Examine the nostrils (nares) themselves.* Is the discharge white and crusty as seen with normal salt secretion, or greenish, yellow and bubbling, as might be seen with an infection? *Examine the mouth next.* Is it closed properly, or are the lips not in contact, with the gums exposed? Are the upper and lower jaws the same length? If closure is poor and the jaws are not the same length, metabolic bone disease with secondary exposure gingivitis, or less commonly, stomatitis, is possible. Gently compress the lower jaw from side to side. If it compresses easily and the eyes protrude slightly, metabolic bone disease (MBD) may be present.

Gently pull on the dewlap to open the mouth. Is the interior of the mouth pale pink, clean, and relatively free of mucus, or is it pasty blue, or swollen with a good deal of mucus or pus? Dental disease or generalized stomatitis may be present if one of these signs is observed. Check the dewlap itself for tears or parasites.

Check the eyes. Are they clear, alertly examining the environment and flush with the head? If not, they may be infected or swollen, or they may be protruding because the bones of the skull are too soft and small, or perhaps, there is an abscess behind the eye.

Examine the ears (tympanic membranes). They should be clear to opaque in color, with a white spot located towards the back of the circular structure. This white spot is the attachment of the extracolumella, a piece of cartilage attached to the columella itself, which is the only bone of the middle ear in reptiles and birds. There should be no evidence of pus, blood or any liquid behind the tympanic membrane. If there is, it might suggest infection or trauma. Look for any evidence of a puncture or tear in the membrane. This is a common occurrence when cats or ferrets attack iguanas. This kind of trauma causes either direct damage to the middle or inner ear, or allows infection to reach the inner ear, so that a loss of balance may result. The quickest way to spot an abnormality of the tympanic membrane and the middle ear is to compare the color on both sides. If one side is clear, and one is opaque, examine the ears (tympanic membrane). They should be clear to opaque in color with a white spot (attachment of the extra columella) located towards the back part.

Examine the pelvic area next. Are the pelvic bones protruding or are they covered with muscle? Protruding pelvic bones suggest <u>chronic</u> malnourishment, not just a few days worth.

Look at the tail and the vent. Is the interior of the vent clean and pale pink or is it crusty and discolored? Is the tail full or very thin, with obvious folds present? The latter also suggests chronic malnourishment. Is the tail complete and flexible right to the tip, or is it broken or very stiff and dry at the end? Are there any unusual lumps and bumps? Is there any retained skin? If so, is there skin anywhere else, particularly the tips of the toes?

Check the overall color and texture of the skin. Generally, it will be similar on both sides. If not, a skin infection may be present. Are there diffuse black spots present? If so, is this lizard housed with other lizards that constantly crawl over each other? Or did the black spots appear since you began your restraint and examination? This would suggest a stress-related change in the distribution of pigment in the skin.

The overall color should be greenish, bluish, grayish, or tan. If it is dark brown or mustard yellow, a serious problem may be present. See the section on color changes.

Once you have completed your examination, make a mental note of the abnormalities you have observed, and refer to those discussions in the *Specific Problems* section of this book.

SPECIFIC PROBLEMS

APPETITE LOSS (ANOREXIA)

Appetite loss is one of the most common problems dealt with by iguana owners. The most common reason for appetite loss is stress associated with an inappropriate environment, or just about any change in the environment. This includes any move from one cage to another, whether it be across the country or across the room. In addition, any time a new iguana is added or removed from an enclosure, an iguana may temporarily stop eating. Remember, the presence of a dominant lizard may suppress the appetite of a submissive one. Anorexia due to environmental stress will usually be resolved once the environment is corrected. Appetite loss due to a move usually lasts about a week.

There are also many medical problems which can cause appetite loss. These include parasites, an intestinal foreign body (your iguana may have swallowed something which is blocking its gut), liver or kidney disease, or gravidity (carrying eggs). Both sexes may become somewhat anorexic during the breeding season.

Hatchling iguanas may have congenital deformities of the gastrointestinal system, or possibly still have some yolk present in the abdominal cavity. Iguanas incubated at temperatures too high may either be physically deformed, or behaviorally abnormal. All of these problems may result in anorexia.

Treatment for anorexia means accurately diagnosing the cause. In the absence of an obvious problem, the help of an experienced reptile veterinarian should be sought. In the meantime, oral fluids and force-feeding may be attempted. If dehydration is suspected, this should be dealt with first (see the section on dehydration), and feeding should be attempted the next day. Strawberry-flavored Ensure® is now considered the force-feeding mixture of choice.

A chronically anorectic iguana. Note the muscle wasting and body appearance.

BITE WOUNDS

Bite wounds fall into two categories: those from other iguanas, and those from cats, dogs, rats, and ferrets. Typically, bites caused by other iguanas consist of multiple small wounds that tend to seal over and become infected with gram-negative bacteria. They have a tendency to become abscesses.

Hence a veterinarian may choose to use slightly different antibiotics when treating bite wounds, depending upon their origin. He/she may recommend a culture and sensitivity to determine a treatment regime. It should be noted that *Clostridium tetani*, the bacteria that causes tetanus in mammals, has been isolated from some abscesses in reptiles. Many other potentially dangerous bacteria have been isolated from these bite wounds.

Bites inflicted by cats and dogs tend to be more severe, often bleed more, and leave open wounds (though not always), and are commonly affected by gram-positive bacteria. They may or may not form abscesses. Dogs and cats have a tendency to pick up small animals and shake them, causing severe internal damage that may not cause much obvious damage on the surface. Under these circumstances, internal bleeding may occur, and sometimes air may enter the wound, abdomen or subcutaneous tissues. This is referred to as emphysema, and it is very serious. In many cases, iguanas without much surface damage have been severely injured and may enter into shock during or soon after the attack. See the sections on bleeding and first aid. Get the iguana to a reptile-oriented veterinarian right away so that the lizard may be treated for shock.

Make no mistake, bites from other iguanas may be severe as well. Many small iguanas are killed by larger iguanas. Prevent this kind of injury by providing secure housing, and only housing compatible iguanas together.

BLEEDING

Ongoing blood loss is an emergency. The flow must be stopped. The best way to stop bleeding is to apply pressure to the affected area. Any absorbent material may be used. Any cotton rag, article of clothing, or gauze sponge may be used for this purpose. If there are no absorbent materials present, simply apply pressure with your bare hand. Usually, after several minutes of pressure, clotting will occur and the bleeding will stop. Exceptions occur if a large artery is injured or in the case of hypocalcemia (a low blood calcium level exists because of poor diet or kidney disease).

Once the bleeding is stopped, a veterinarian may be consulted for further advice or treatment. Small wounds may require nothing more than one or two applications of a topical antibiotic such as povidone-iodine solution (Betadine®). Large wounds may require suturing and injectable antibiotics.

Certainly, if bleeding cannot be stopped, continue applying pressure at the site of the injury and rush the iguana to a veterinarian immediately. Bleeding from the mouth or colon should also be considered an emergency and warrant an emergency visit to the veterinarian.

Bleeding from a toenail that has been clipped too short or torn off is a different kind of problem. Often, pressure will not stop bleeding in these cases. However, a number of household items will. Any particulate substance like flour, gelatin, or baking soda may be applied to a bleeding nail and will often help it clot. If these are not handy, try jamming the bleeding claw into a bar of soap temporarily. If you can't stop the bleeding, apply pressure and rush the iguana to a veterinarian.

A veterinarian may use a pressure bandage, a clotting agent such as ferric subsulphate, or electrocautery to stop the bleeding.

BROKEN TAIL

One of the most common traumatic events in the lives of iguanas is complete or partial breakage of the tail. The independent movement of the tail and the hemorrhage that accompany this event are often very frightening to the owner and often send them into a state of panic. The first step is to calm down. Tail autotomy, which is the voluntary breakage and movement of the tail, is a natural occurrence in the family Iguanidae. It is a basically a defensive strategy in which a potential predator is distracted by the moving tail long enough to allow the escape of the prey, in this case, the iguana. And while it may not be a pretty sight, the iguana is usually not in immediate danger of dying if the bleeding stops. A clotting disorder might result in a severe problem under these circumstances, but this is extremely rare. In most cases, the exposed muscle fibers and blood vessels contract immediately and stop the bleeding within a minute. If not, apply pressure to the bleeding area immediately. Sometimes, a short term pressure bandage using a cling type bandage material will help, but this should usually be removed within 12 hours. Once the bleeding stops, apply an antiseptic for a day or two, then stop. Some antiseptics may actually delay healing. It may also be helpful to house the iguana on a non-sticking substrate for a week or so i.e. newspaper instead of wood chips. Tail regrowth will usually occur in a well-fed lizard, as long as the tail was broken at a fracture plane, not between vertebrae. Should the tail not start regenerating, you may wish to consult a veterinarian, who will examine the diet and environment, and consider the possibility of rebreaking the tail (with anesthesia) at a fracture plane, so that it regenerates properly. When regeneration begins the tail is usually very dark, and often points upward. It usually lightens in colors and straightens out as it grows.

Regenerated tail

Forked tail

BURNS

Unfortunately, burns are extremely common in iguanas. The most frequent location for burns is on the abdomen, but they can occur anywhere. Ventral heat sources, notably hot rocks are most commonly incriminated. Heat lamps are also likely to cause burns, and these burns, along the back and sides may be severe. Iguanas may hug heat sources so closely during cold weather that they literally cook muscles to the point that they peel off the ribs. So unless you like your iguana well done, you should use heat sources carefully. Burns usually appear as patches of darkly colored skin.

Treatment involves: 1) Removing the source of the burn 2) Topical antibiotics 3) Injectable antibiotics. A veterinarian should be consulted in cases of severe burns. Debridement of necrotic tissue and knowledgeable bandaging may be necessary.

TOPICALS THAT WORK
WELL ON BURNS

1) Polysporin®
2) Neosporin®
3) Betadine Ointment®
4) Silvadine Cream®
5) Bactine ®

Lateral burn, from a heat lamp. Owners tend to underestimate the heat produced by lamps.

COLD EXPOSURE

Unexpected exposure to cold is a very common problem. Millions of iguanas are now housed in climates far cooler than their tropical origins. When they fall asleep near a poorly insulated window, experience a power outage during cold weather or far worse, escape to the outside, cold exposure is a likely occurrence.

The seriousness of the condition will depend upon several factors. The general health, size and acclimatization (how much cold has the iguana been exposed to previously and for how long) will all determine how it responds to cold exposure.

Typically, exposure to low temperatures will result in a loss of normal reflexes and normal circulatory function will be compromised. An iguana near its critical thermal minimum temperature (low temperature at which death occurs) will actually appear dead. Indeed, it will not be able to right itself should it be flipped over on its back; it will have no response to stimuli, and perform almost entirely imperceptible breathing. The heartbeat may just be barely observable behind the left or right arm. In any case, bring the iguana into a warm room and start to warm it up **SLOWLY!** Do not assume that it is dead until after you have warmed it up for 4 or 5 hours and still seen no signs of life.

DO NOT PLACE THE IGUANA DIRECTLY OVER THE CENTER OF A HEATING PAD OR DIRECTLY UNDER A HEAT LAMP! Heat sources may be used, but they should be gentle heat sources i.e. warm water in bottles, an incandescent bulb that produces a warm, not hot area. Gentle massage to the arms, legs, and tail may help to improve circulation. Do not do this if any body parts appear to have been frozen however, as this may worsen the damage. Sometimes the tail may be lifted up temporarily to increase the blood flow back to the heart. Call your veterinarian immediately and explain the situation. He/she may wish to examine the lizard as soon as possible and administer anti-shock therapy, which will usually include fluids, antibiotics and steroids. This may save your iguana's life.

Within an hour or so, reflexes should start returning to your iguana. Breathing and a heartbeat should become obvious, and over several hours the grogginess should wear off. Even if improvement is seen immediately upon warming, the iguana should still be seen by a veterinarian, who may still wish to administer antibiotics and fluids. Remember that a severe respiratory infection may occur following a chill, and realize that it may take days or weeks to develop. Antibiotics may help to prevent this and are almost always indicated for cold exposure. Antibiotics will also help if freezing damage to the toes or tail tip is present. Surgery may be required as well but this will take several days to determine.

COLOR CHANGE

A lthough not as variable in color as are the true chameleons, iguanas do change color a great deal. Slow changes in color, such as from dark green to light green or grayish green, are usually a reaction to light intensity and heat associated with thermoregulation and photophase (length of day). The gradual color is also true with the orange wash, particularly in male iguanas during breeding season. Some slow color changes occur with maturity i.e. the change from bright green to grayish green as an iguana matures.

Rapid color changes are often a sign of infection or trauma, but may simply be stress related. As mentioned previously, gray or brown patches may indicate a burn.

Mustard yellow is often considered the color of death in iguanas. It may be caused by a shock-associated situation. In shock, circulation to the skin is poor, and in iguanas, this makes the skin, especially ventrally, develop a yellowish wash. Certainly, there are other factors (i.e. jaundice) which will produce a yellowish discoloration, but these are much less common than shock.

A generalized dark brown color usually suggests that an iguana is experiencing pain, often of an abdominal origin. Examples would include the ingestion of a poisonous plant, a foreign body obstruction, or an intessuception (the gut folding over itself like a sock turned partially inside out). This discoloration may rapidly turn to yellowish discoloration as the pain leads to a shock condition.

Both mustard yellow and generalized brown discoloration indicates probable emergencies. The iguana should be rushed to a reptile veterinarian immediately. The veterinarian will administer anti-shock therapy and possibly consider emergency surgery. In such situations, there may not be time to perform the usual diagnostics such as a barium study, but each situation will need to be evaluated individually. Large patches of red discoloration, or generalized redness suggest either a burn or infection. Such an infection would be very serious, since the bacteria involved are likely to have entered the bloodstream. This condition is referred to a septicemia, and injectable antibiotics are needed immediately if the iguana is to recover.

CONSTIPATION

Most iguanas defecate every one to three days. If this period is exceeded the owner needs to be concerned that their pet may be constipated. Frequently, the inability to defecate may be associated with other problems. These include bloating, anorexia, intestinal parasitism, kidney disease or imminent egg-laying. Some iguanas seem to literally "cook" the stool in the colon when they hug ventral heat sources during periods of cold.

Often, chronically constipated iguanas will have a history of metabolic bone disease. I suspect that these animals may have experienced some loss of gut muscle tone during this disease, due in part to hypocalcemia (low blood levels of calcium). This loss of muscle tone may later result in poor passage rates and predispose these animals to constipation. This problem is especially common in those animals with fractured spines, which suggests that a neurological deficit may be involved as well.

In all cases of constipation, the first step in treatment is to administer a shallow, warm soak. This often will stimulate defecation without any other treatment. If this fails the first time, repeat for a period of one half hour per day for 3 or 4 days. Laxatives may also be attempted and I have successfully used small amounts of cat fur-ball medicine on some of my patients. Administer 1 drop to one-fourth teaspoon of this laxative to the back of the mouth for 2 or 3 days in a row and wait several days. If the warm water soaks and oral laxatives don't work, it's time to seek professional advice.

A reptile veterinarian may consider taking radiographs to rule out foreign bodies, perform a fecal exam to rule out parasites and then administer an enema to provide some relief. The warm, soapy water enema may be followed by gentle but firm abdominal pressure in order to start expelling fecal matter and in some cases uric acid deposits. Some individuals have successfully stimulated iguanas to defecate by rubbing the abdominal area with a warm, wet rag.

Of course, the underlying cause for the constipation must be addressed or the problem will return.

DEHYDRATION

The presence of dehydration (insufficient body fluid) is recognized in iguanas by signs similar to those used to diagnose dehydration in other animals. Basically, these signs include sunken eyes, loose wrinkled skin which when tented does not return to its original position, and dry, often sticky or mucousy membranes in the mouth. Small iguanas feel particularly light, and skin usually appears very dry. Sometimes there is a good deal of retained skin. In many cases, dehydration is associated with starvation, and muscle wasting is also evident.

Treatment for dehydration includes either injectable or oral fluids or both. Diluted Pedialyte®, diluted Gatorade® or preferably, Reptilaid® are good oral rehydration solutions. In cases of severe dehydration, injectable fluids may be indicated. These fluids include .9% NaCL, and 2.5% dextrose with .45% NaCL.

The following chart shows approximate fluid amounts to be given per day to different size iguanas. These are maintenance amounts and severely dehydrated iguanas may require more, up to double the amount shown.

WEIGHT (GRAMS/LBS)	DOSE (ML)
10	½
20	½
30	1
40	1
50	1
60	2
70	2
80	2
90	2
100	2
200	4
300	6
400	9
454 / 1 lb	10
500 / 1.1 lb	10
1,000 / 2.2 lb	20
2,000 / 4.4 lb	40
3,000 / 6.6 lb	60

DENTAL DISEASE AND STOMATITIS
(MOUTH ROT)

Iguanas and other lizards in captivity frequently develop mouth infections, although this condition is not nearly as common as it is in snakes. Increased salivation, redness, swelling, and pus pockets in the mouth are the cardinal signs of stomatitis. If the iguana is also breathing with some difficulty, it may have pneumonia as well. The two conditions may occur together.

One must be careful to distinguish stomatitis from exposure gingivitis however. The latter condition occurs almost exclusively in cases of advanced Metabolic Bone Disease (or as a sequelae to MBD, even if it is the healing stage). As the jaws bend and bow outward, the gums are exposed to the air, dry out, and become inflamed. See under *Protrusions.*

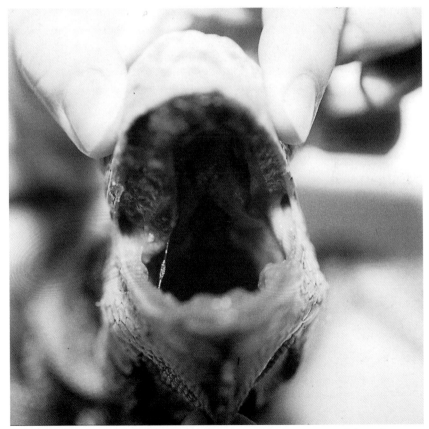

Stomatitis. This severe stomatitis cultured out *Salmonella*. This points out that bites from iguanas can be serious.

Unless the exposure is corrected or the tissues protected, no antibiotic known will solve this problem. The treatment for exposure gingivitis usually requires correction of the underlying MBD, which is discussed in other areas of this book, and possibly the use of some topical protectant/antibiotic. Both KY Jelly® and Silvadine Cream® have worked extremely well. Another product which has been effective in treating exposure gingivitis and mild stomatitis is Maxiguard Oral Gel®. Silvadine® is also an excellent topical antibiotic if the exposed tissue appears to be infected. Simply apply one of these products to the exposed area with a cotton applicator once per day. If left untreated, or treated the wrong way, exposure gingivitis may progress to severe stomatitis, which is much more difficult to eliminate. Again, no antibiotics will be helpful if the exposure is not corrected.

True stomatitis can be very difficult to eliminate. Deep pus pockets and a great deal of swelling may require prolonged antibiotic therapy and regular debridement (cutting away necrotic tissue). Topical povidone-iodine solution (e.g. Betadine®) or chlorhexidine solution should be applied daily. If radiographs (X-rays) reveal bone destruction, the infection has spread to the bone. This is called osteomyelitis, and it is likely that six to eight weeks of antibiotic therapy may be necessary. Antibiotics such as Ceftazidime are effective and relatively non-toxic. Your veterinarian will discuss options. Remember that some anesthesia may be necessary to properly clean and debride the mouth, especially at first.

A recent study indicated that soft, mushy diets, possibly containing large amounts of fruits, may predispose iguanas to dental disease and stomatitis. Hence, increasing the amount of greens and reducing the amount of fruits should be considered for two major reasons. Firstly, the high calcium content will reduce the likelihood for MBD to occur, and secondly, more greens will probably mean less stomatitis.

DERMATITIS (SKIN INFECTION)

Any change in color or texture of an iguana's skin could indicate an infection, but can occur secondary to a burn. These changes may include black spots, brown spots, dry or moist patches. They may even include areas of depigmentation (areas where the green color is lost). Unfortunately, these changes are usually not very specific to a particular disease organism. This means that many different bacterial or fungal organisms could produce similar signs. Hence, while home treatment may be attempted, it will at best be an educated guess as to what you are treating. A veterinarian will often perform cultures on suspicious skin lesions in order to determine the cause and to determine the best treatment to prescribe.

Additionally, it is important to remember that skin infections, whether they are bacterial or fungal, are usually secondary to some environmental problem, such as trauma, excessive cage moisture, parasites, or a burn. These must be corrected prior to treating any skin infection.

Once the environmental factors are corrected, attempted home treatment of suspicious spots may be attempted with a number of topical medications. Antibiotic ointments such as Polysporin® or Betadine® have been effective. Silvadine Cream® is an outstanding topical for both primary bacterial infections and burns. Should a fungal infection be suspected, topical ointments such as Tinactin®, Lotrimin® or Veltrim® may be used, and have worked well. Betadine® ointment has antifungal activity as well as antibacterial activity. Topical vitamins A and E, as well as Aloe Vera extract have also been used with some success on skin lesions in lizards. Reptile skin heals slowly and may require daily applications for over a month, regardless of the topical chosen.

Remember, that severe skin infections may be life-threatening, and systemic (injectable) antibiotics may be indicated as well. See the sections on *Parasites* (mites), *Burns, Facial abrasions* and *Lumps and bumps.*

DIARRHEA

Diarrhea is defined as the occurrence of loose, watery, often foul smelling stools. As in mammals, it may be caused by a variety of things, including bacteria, protozoans, metazoans (i.e. worms), inappropriate diet, or abnormal gut function.

Acute diarrhea (diet with a rapid onset that has not lasted a long time) may be managed conservatively by using Kaopectate® or other protecting/coating agents and also by the simple act of withholding food for 24 hours. A dose of 1 ml per kilogram (1/2 ml per pound) is often effective.

Chronic diarrhea (diarrhea lasting more than two days) is a much more serious problem. Fluids replacement is the first and most important consideration. Diluted Gatorade® or Pedialyte® or preferably Reptilaid® given orally at the rate recommended in the table in the section on dehydration will be very helpful. Once again, Kaopectate may also be helpful. However, in chronic diarrhea, a cause must be determined in order to effect a cure. A veterinarian must perform a fecal exam (possibly repeated fecal exams), and possibly a fecal culture in order to determine a possible etiology (cause) of the diarrhea. In cases where no parasites or pathogenic bacteria are isolated, other causes of diarrhea may be suspected. A foreign body, partial intestinal blockage, poor diet (not enough fiber, too much fruit), or tumor may be possible. A radiograph (X-ray) may be suggested by your veterinarian if nothing

A dehydrated iguana. Note the skin folds and tenting of the skin.

is obvious after pathogenic organisms have been ruled out and the diet has been corrected, if the diarrhea persists. Remember that the proper diet is usually one that is fairly high in fiber and low in fruits. See the section on *Basic Care in Captivity* for dietary suggestions.

Be patient. Chronic diarrhea is a complicated problem and reptiles heal slowly. After antibiotic therapy is over (if antibiotics were chosen), sometimes a veterinarian will recommend an unusual follow up therapy. This is feeding the fresh feces of another parasite free iguana to your iguana. The purpose of this is to re-inoculate your iguana's gastrointestinal tract with normal bacteria, which will aid in the digestive process and hopefully help stop the diarrhea.

Some veterinarians have also recommended the use of a product called Lactaid® following the use of antibiotics. This product is primarily an enzyme supplement, and while it may not help that much, it probably wont hurt either. Its effectiveness has been questioned by a number of veterinarians.

In the meantime, make sure to disinfect your iguana's enclosure regularly, and provide a suitable captive environment and the proper diet.

DROWNING

Iguanas are excellent swimmers and climbers and rarely drown, however situations may arise when an iguana falls into a pool and is unable to scale the steep sides or gets tangled in something under the water. Upon finding an iguana in a pool, immediately remove it and evaluate its condition. Is it alert and breathing, or is it unconscious, and possibly not breathing at all? In either case, immediately hold the head downward and observe for water running out of the mouth or nose. Any water running out at all suggests the possibility of fluid in the lungs (although it is possible that the iguana just drank a large amount of water). Fresh water is particularly damaging to the lungs and often results in a secondary infection several days or weeks afterwards ....even if the iguana looks perfectly normal. Have the lizard examined immediately by a veterinarian. He/she will probably administer a course of injectable antibiotic and possibly a drug such as atropine or aminophylline (a drying agent and bronchodilator respectively). The doses are listed in the section entitled *Medicines*. Keep the iguana very warm after such an incident.

It is very difficult to determine if an iguana is dead under these circumstances. A veterinarian may be able to detect a heartbeat, intubate (place a tube in the trachea) and resuscitate the iguana.

DYSTOCIA (EGG BINDING)

When female iguanas reach a size large enough to lay eggs, they are possible candidates for dystocia (egg binding). Once the snout to vent length is approximately 9 inches, they can form eggs. If these females have not been with a male, they will be infertile eggs, but nevertheless, they can form eggs.

Problems usually arise when younger, smaller females receive enough nutrition to form these eggs but not enough calcium to place shells around these eggs, or enough calcium to have the strength to lay them without assistance.

This problem may be recognized by a combination of physical and behavioral signs. Typically, there is a loss of appetite followed by (or accompanying) a gradual swelling of the abdomen. The swelling eventually takes on a lumpy appearance, even though this is not always discernible. An iguana may also begin pacing the cage, digging at the bottom with its front feet and many iguanas may traumatize their toes and noses severely in an attempt to escape or find the right place to deposit the eggs.

If you suspect that egg-laying is imminent the following steps are advised.

1) Provide a suitable nesting site. This is discussed in more detail in *the Green Iguana Manual*, but is described briefly here. See below.

2) Offer food regularly but do not be alarmed if very little is consumed. Offer food by hand every day. These few bits might be all that your iguana eats for the entire second half of her gestation (gravid period).

3) Disturb as little as possible. Do not change the environment any more than is necessary with the exception of adding the egg-laying box. Don't add any new animals. Consider removing cagemates if they are aggressive toward the gravid female or she becomes aggressive toward them.

If you are certain that the female is gravid, or are uncertain if you even have a female, take your anorectic iguana to a veterinarian that treats reptiles. He/she will evaluate your lizard in order to determine:
1) Is it a female?
2) Is she gravid?
3) Is there another medical problem causing the anorexia?
4) Is any medical intervention required?

Generally speaking, medical or surgical intervention is not indicated if the iguana is <u>strong</u>, <u>alert</u>, and <u>feeding ever so slightly</u> (S.A.F.E). If she becomes weak, appears depressed, becomes totally anorectic, or starts laying eggs, then stops suddenly, a veterinarian may choose to intervene medically or surgically. Medical intervention includes chemical induction of egg-laying, and this usually consists of three things.

Firstly, fluids may be administered intraperitoneally to correct dehydration and assist in moistening the uterus. Secondly calcium may be administered to improve muscle tone. Lastly oxytocin (or vasotocin) is administered to stimulate uterine contractions and expulsion of the eggs.

Doses of drugs used for the chemical induction of oviposition

Fluids (sterile): 2.5% Dextrose in .45% Sodium Chloride - 20 ml/kg/ day I.P.(Intraperiotoneally / intracoelemically). Aspirate before injection to make sure the needle is not in the colon, bladder, or an egg.

Calcium: Calphosan® -1 ml/kg/12 hours as needed for egg-laying.

Oxytocin: 5-10 IU every 4-6 hours for 1-2 days. If no eggs are laid or egg-laying starts and then stops, surgery may be necessary. These shots are not without risk, because the uterus may be torn if the eggs are adhered to it when muscle contractions begin.

Surgical intervention is called for in cases of severe depression or metabolic bone disease. Your veterinarian will probably want to run some blood work in order to determine blood calcium, phosphorus and uric acid levels, as well as taking radiographs prior to considering surgery.

Two surgical options are available. The best and most logical choice is a complete ovariohysterectomy, which involves the removal of the uterus and all of the eggs contained within, as well as both ovaries. Not only is this a faster surgery, but it also eliminates the problem in the future.
The second option, which is rarely performed anymore, is a c-section. This involves multiple slices in paper-thin uterus, and the "milking out" of up to 60 eggs! The uterus then needs to be re-sutured, making the entire procedure extremely tedious. The risk for hemorrhage, infection and reoccurrence of egg-binding are obviously much greater with this procedure than the latter.

Thus, dystocia is a complicated and serious problem that often requires medical expertise in order to correct. Both medical and surgical routes are valuable, albeit time consuming. Be aware that it often takes more time spay an iguana than it does to spay a large dog (or two)! Hence, the procedure is justifiably expensive. Remember that spayed iguanas make excellent and long-lived pets. They may live 20 or more years.

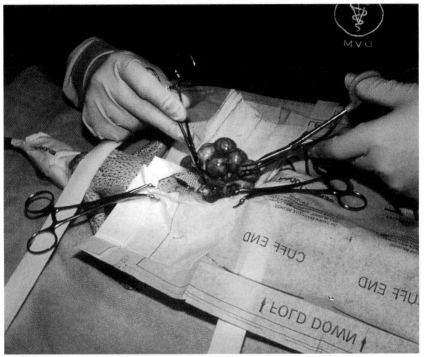

Spaying a female green iguana will eliminate the risks of dystocia in the future.

EYE PROBLEMS

Any abnormalities of the eyes are considered medical problems which should receive professional attention immediately. These abnormalities include: cloudiness, bleeding, punctures, protrusions, redness, or apparent blindness. Red or "bloodshot" eyes are particularly worrisome as they often suggest septicemia (bacteria in the blood) or toxemia (toxins in the blood).

In the absence of immediate veterinary help, one should keep the affected eye(s) moist using any over the counter eyewash solution. A topical OPHTHALMIC ANTIBIOTIC OINTMENT or SOLUTION (eye drops) **WITHOUT STEROIDS** may be used on the eye(s) if no veterinary care is available for a prolonged period of time. Otherwise, keep the eye(s) moist and do not apply an antibiotic, in case the veterinarian wants to perform a culture and sensitivity of the eye(s) or surrounding structures. Topical antibiotics would destroy the effectiveness of this test and might hide the true causative agent (bacteria) of the infection.

In the case of severe trauma to the eye, with rupture of the globe, or severe infection of the eye, a veterinarian may suggest removal of the eye. This is called an enucleation, and will actually reduce the pain the iguana is likely to be experiencing. Remember, in almost all cases that this procedure is recommended, the eye is non-visual i.e. the iguana cannot see out of the eye. I have seen a number of one-eyed iguanas do very well in captivity. Even a totally blind iguana may be able to adjust well to a stable cage environment and find food, although they do better when supplemented with regular hand feedings. Again, when eye(s) problems are first noticed, have your iguana see your veterinarian immediately.

Eye problems may be serious. This swelling of the lid may have resulted from trauma, and the infection may spread to the eye itself if left untreated.

FACIAL (ROSTRAL) ABRASIONS

One of the most common and serious injuries of iguanas, particularly those middle-sized iguanas which have been recently imported, is trauma to the rostral area (nose). Basically, these iguanas are running head first into invisible walls (i.e. glass) and are severely traumatizing themselves. Some of these injuries are disfiguring and startling to observe as the entire skin surface from the front of the face may be missing and bone and teeth are exposed.

The first step in treating this kind of lesion is to stop the iguana from crashing into these walls. Housing the affected iguana singly, in a large cage, in a quiet area will help tremendously. Next, make the barriers visible. There are no invisible barriers in a tropical forest. Hence, painting the lower part of a glass enclosure, or covering the lower part with some sort of paper, will usually slow down or stop the "crashing". For some iguanas it is helpful to crumple up some newspaper and place it in the bottom of the cage, especially next to the sides. Not only does this create a visual barrier, but it increases the number of hiding places for the iguana, and actually forms a soft physical barrier that makes crashing into the wall nearly impossible. In fact, many frightened iguanas may just drop from their perch into the crumpled newspapers and remain motionless, rather than taking off at high speeds.

Rostral abrasion. Rough-sided cages and large, recently imported iguanas do not mix. Use smooth-sided enclosures and create visual barriers so they don't run into clear glass.

After changing the environment to reduce the likelihood of crashing into it, the facial injuries may be treated. As with many skin lesions in iguanas, topical antibacterial ointments or creams work better than solutions. Betadine® ointment or Silvadine Cream® have worked very well under these circumstances. In severe cases, systemic (injectable) antibiotics may also be necessary or helpful. Frequently, a dark crust will form over the injured area (a scab), and this will be lost as the tissue underneath heals. A bed of granulation tissue (vascular and fibrous tissue) will often form first, and this will soon be covered by scar tissue. The granulation tissue usually appears pink colored and rough, and may "seep" serum, so it appears moist as well. The "raw" area will gradually be covered by "whitish" or gray, smooth and often shiny scar tissue. Generally speaking, if you control the infection and take care of proper nutrition, the iguana will heal just fine. Once the face is healed, the major concern will be the patency of the nares. In other words, have the nostrils become closed by scar tissue? If they have, corrective surgery may be helpful. One last note: an iguana with this kind of injury, or in this kind of stress, may not eat readily. Force-feeding may be needed. See the sections on *Anorexia, Dehydration* and *First Aid.*

FAILURE TO GROW

Young iguanas should grow rapidly. Failure to triple in size in the first year is an indicator that either the diet or the lighting/heating is incorrect. An iguana should reach a snout vent length of at least 6 inches (21 cm) by one year of age. Failure to do may also suggest a gastrointestinal problem, such as malabsorption (poor absorption of food from the gut), or more likely, intestinal parasitism. Work first on correcting the diet and lighting, and then check with a veterinarian.

Remember that most cases of poor growth are associated with signs of MBD as well.

Classic MBD. All signs are present in this spiny-tailed iguana.

FRACTURES

A bone is definitely broken if you see a splintered bone fragment sticking through the skin. This is a compound fracture, and this is an immediate medical emergency. Rush the lizard to a veterinarian right away. Place the lizard in a dark clean box for transportation. **Don't put any ointments or creams on the wound! You may flush the wound with hydrogen peroxide, or dilute providone-iodine solution (1/5 iodine to water).** Generally speaking, most people have a hard time immobilizing their pet iguana enough to put a temporary splint on, and usually do more harm than good. Therefore, applying a splint is not recommended for transport to the veterinarian.

A bone **MAY** be broken if any or all of the following signs are observed: 1) The iguana is not using the leg or the arm. 2) The leg or arm is bent in an unusual position or else is dangling. 3) The leg or arm is swollen. 4) The leg or arm is shorter on one side than the leg or arm on the other side.

In situations 1 and 2, you should seek veterinary advice immediately, while in 3 and 4, seek veterinary help as soon as possible. The latter two presentations are usually more stable fractures, which reduces the likelihood of further injury, and makes them less immediate problems. Nevertheless, all iguanas suspected of having a fracture should be examined as soon as possible, and kept quiet in the meantime. Little or no handling is recommended at the time, and one may wish to cover the cage until the examination by the veterinarian.

Depending upon the type of fracture and the bone involved, as well as the nutritional status of the animal, bones will heal differently. Most fractures can be managed conservatively (i.e. with cage rest, confinement). Some will require some sort of fixation (i.e. cast, splint or pin). Your veterinarian will usually want to take a radiograph in order to determine the type of fracture present and the status of the skeleton. If the bones are very thin, as in metabolic bone disease (MBD), a pathological fracture (i.e. fracture associated with very little stress) is likely and two things are obvious. Firstly, fixation devices may not work and may actually make the situation worse. Secondly, correcting the underlying thinness of the bones will do far more good than any fixation device. Thus, many veterinarians including myself frequently recommend vitamin and calcium injections and supplements, as well as dietary and lighting changes rather than braces and pins for broken legs, when MBD is involved.

Shockingly, many iguanas will start using their broken legs within one week if they are treated properly.

A fractured spine is a much more serious problem. Move slowly around these animals and handle them carefully. One vigorous whip of the tail could seriously injure the spinal cord. See the discussion under *Paralysis*.

IM vitamin injection in base of tail. Antibiotics are usually administered in the front half of the body.

HEAD TILT, CIRCLING AND LOSS OF BALANCE

If an iguana experiences trauma to the head or has a middle/inner ear infection, it may develop a head tilt to one side, or begin circling to one side, or both. If the eyes are moving like windshield wipers, in a regular back and forth motion (called nystagmus by veterinarians), then damage to part of the brain is also likely.

A veterinarian should be consulted immediately in any case of head tilt or circling. They may administer powerful anti-inflammatory agents called steroids, which may reduce the likelihood of permanent brain damage. Where infection is suspected, such as after a bite injury to the head, antibiotics are also indicated.

The prognosis depends upon the cause and the severity, but many cases will recover if given enough time. It may take several months for any improvement to take place in some cases, and force-feeding may be required for this entire period.

Head tilt. This iguana had an object fall on it. It recovered fairly quickly after a visit to the vet following several steroid injections.

LAMENESS (LIMPING)

As in mammals, lameness in iguanas may have a multitude of causes. Soft tissue injuries, dislocations and fractures are all possible. Metabolic problems such as a vitamin B deficiency or MBD related problems, neoplasia (tumors) or osteomyelitis (bone infection) have also been determined to be causes of lameness.

Generally speaking, there is little you can do at home to diagnose lameness. Many cases of lameness will respond to several days of cage rest and a high quality diet, however, this is potentially risky if the problem is related to an infection, neoplasia or severe metabolic problem. In most cases, it is usually better to take a radiograph (X-ray) and have a veterinarian prescribe an effective course of treatment.

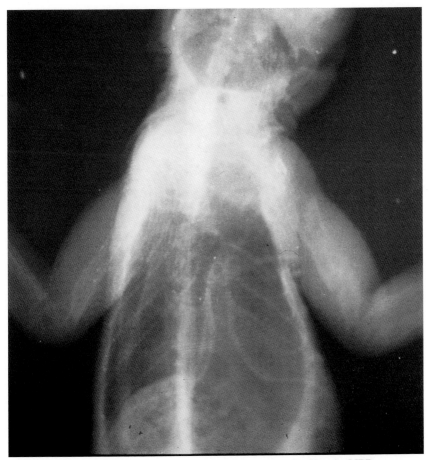

Radiograph showing poor bone density, a common finding in MBD.

LUMPS AND BUMPS

Lumps and bumps of varying sizes are one of the most common reasons that iguanas are presented to veterinarians. These lumps and bumps are usually abscesses or granulomas, which are pus- filled pockets. They may also be tumors or cysts, but these are quite less common. In either case, veterinary help should be sought, since anesthesia and surgery are usually called for. See the section on *Swelling*, particularly the discussion on swelling of the skin for more details on treatment.

Abscesses. Solid pus requires a large incision to remove. Sedation is usually required. Sometimes excess skin around the abscess may need to be removed as well.

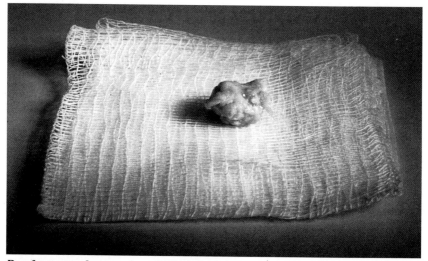

Pus from an abscess. As mentioned elsewhere, reptile pus is usually solid, not liquid.

NAIL TRIMMING AND TORN NAILS

NAIL TRIMMING

Long sharp claws may injure the owner and iguana alike. Nail trimmings on large iguanas may be accomplished with standard dog and cat nail trimmers, while small iguanas may have nails trimmed with human nail trimmers or suture scissors.

In the last several years the demand for other methods of protecting owners from their iguanas sharp claws has lead to the use of Soft Paws® and surgical declawing, as seen in cats. Soft Paws® are small plastic caps that are glued on slightly trimmed nails using a cyanoacrylate glue. They last approximately six months. Surgical declawing has been described in a veterinary journal, but at the time of this writing is not commonly performed.

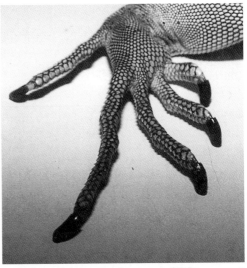

Soft Paws® are plastic caps which prevent trauma to both other iguanas and the owner. The only drawback is that the iguanas can't climb as well.

TORN NAILS

Iguanas frequently break or tear their nails off. The immediate concern is usually bleeding. Apply some pressure and see the section on bleeding. The nail may or may not regenerate depending upon how much of the nail base was torn off. Correct the flaw in the cage that led to the injury, keep the nails trimmed, and this kind of injury is unlikely to reoccur. Remember that iguanas with missing claws seem to do just fine.

Owners of medium to large iguanas need to exercise some caution when handling iguanas. See the section on handling. Their sharp claws can cause severe, infected lacerations. Wash every wound with hydrogen peroxide and follow with a good antibacterial soap. Immediate cleansing could prevent a major infection later.

OVERHEATING

The first indication that an iguana may be getting close to over heating is open mouth breathing or <u>panting</u>. Make no mistake however, many iguanas choose to become so hot that they pant. High body temperatures allow them to digest food rapidly and fight off some infections. One must realize however, that they are choosing temperatures dangerously close to the upper limit of their POTR (Preferred Optimum Temperature Range), possibly even higher, near the CTMAX (Critical Thermal Maximum Temperature), the high temperature at which death occurs! If they choose such a temperature and something goes wrong i.e. they are unable to escape when they are ready to, they may die within 5 minutes (300 seconds)! Heat kills by denaturing enzymes (cooking). It is quick and it is irreversible. Many a herpetoculturist has wished to have the last 5 minutes back. Don't be one of them.

If one finds an iguana limp and very hot to the touch, overheating is the most likely cause. Immediately, get the iguana out of the direct sunlight, and if possible run cool (room temperature) water over its body. Do not use ice water or ice. If there is any response at all including movement, breathing or blinking, get the iguana to a veterinarian immediately. He/she may administer steroids and fluids to counteract shock and reduce the likelihood of brain damage, which is a distinct possibility. See the discussion on *Dehydration*, a condition which may accompany overheating.

PARALYSIS AND PARESIS (WEAKNESS)

One of the most frightening signs an iguana owner can observe is the sudden onset of paralysis. Typically, a young iguana one to three years old suddenly develops total or partial loss of function of the hind legs. The most common reason this occurs is a spinal fracture and resultant compression of the spinal cord, often secondary to metabolic bone disease (MBD). Also possible, but far less common causes include vitamin and mineral deficiencies and toxicities.

The prognosis, of course, depends upon the cause. Severe spinal cord trauma with resultant bladder and bowel distention has the poorest prognosis, while vitamin deficiencies and toxicities have the best prognosis.

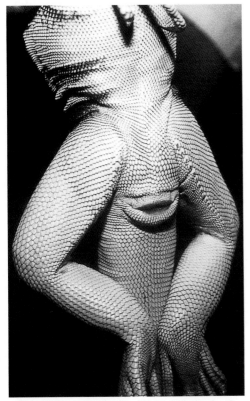

In any case, a veterinarian should be consulted immediately, and no hasty decisions should be made. Young iguanas have a tremendous ability to heal and **should always be given several weeks or longer to heal.** This is especially true in cases where the iguana responds favorably to a deep pain test (a toe pinch) with more than a reflex response (i.e. the iguana is aware of the pinch and actively does something to indicate it). And certainly the prognosis for recovery from rear limb paresis (weakness) is much better than for rear limb paralysis (loss of voluntary function).

Treatment may include vitamins Bl and D3, calcium, glucose, and most importantly, time. See the *Medicine* section for doses.

Hind limb paralysis. The prognosis for recovery is unknown. Consult with your veterinarian and give it some time. Note the atonic cloaca (i.e. there is no muscle tone around the cloaca).

PARASITES (WORMS, MITES, PROTO-ZOANS, AND HARMFUL BACTERIA)

Generally speaking, captive iguanas seem to have few parasites when compared with other reptile species. Nevertheless, oxyurids (pinworms) are extremely common and may cause intestinal problems in untreated iguanas. Problems associated with these worms include diarrhea, constipation, obstruction of the colon resulting in bloating, or just a very irritable iguana. Rarely, severe colitis (inflammation of the colon) may occur, resulting in the death of the affected iguana. Many iguanas are asymptomatic, however (i.e. they have the worms but show no signs). Indeed, over 90% of the young iguanas examined have these worms. Many long-term captives are heavily loaded with these parasites and their owners are entirely unaware of them. Successful treatment involves the administration of an effective deworming agent like fenbendazole 50-100 mg/kg by mouth (Repeated in 2 weeks and again 2 weeks later). This should be followed by a negative fecal exam (3-6 months later). Regular (annual) fecal exams should be performed thereafter.

Mites, particularly lizard mites *Herstiella trombidiiforms* occur occasionally in iguanas and typically cause bilaterally symmetrical lesions (equal on both sides). Typically, these lesions include dark patches on the wrists, ankles, axillary (armpit) and inguinal (upper thigh and groin) areas, as well as many spots ventrally (on the belly). Adult mites look similar to snakes mites to the naked eye, but move much faster. Microscopically they have much narrower and more pointed heads than do snakes mites. The latter rarely infect iguanas.

Treatments have varied from painting the lizard with any vegetable oil once a day for several weeks (which suffocates the mites) to spraying the lizard with dilute ivermectin spray every 3 days for 3 weeks. The ivermectin spray is produced by adding ½ cc of the Ivomec® concentrate to 1 quart (approximately 1 liter) of water and shaking well. Regardless of the treatment used, the entire cage must be cleaned and disinfected or the mites will come right back . Wooden objects are especially likely to harbor mites so they require special care, namely cooking (300°F for 15 minutes) or soaking (several hours to days in dilute bleach water).

Lizard mite lesions. Note the bilaterally (equally distributed) symmetrical appearance.

Pathogenic (disease-causing) protozoans, namely amoeba and flagellates, are commonly found in the stool of sick iguanas and may be either the cause of gastrointestinal signs, or secondary to another problem, such as gut stasis or bacterial overgrowth. Flagyl® (metronidazole) at a dose of 50-100 mg/kg is the drug of choice for eliminating these parasites. The dose must be repeated in two weeks and the cage must be thoroughly cleaned and disinfected in the meantime.

Bacterial overgrowth of the gut, especially with known pathogenic organisms, such as *Salmonella, Campylobacter*, and others is certainly a possible case of gastrointestinal disease. Signs include diarrhea, bloating, anorexia and abdominal pain. Oral and injectable antibiotics, based upon a culture and sensitivity may be indicated in some cases. However, many veterinarians prefer not to treat known cases of *Salmonella* because they do not wish to contribute to the development of antibiotic resistant strains.

Your veterinarian will be able to diagnose the cause and choose the best treatment plan for your iguana parasite problem.

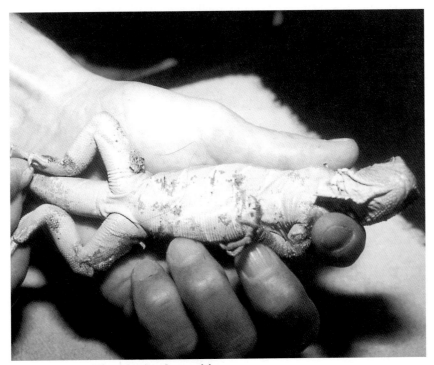

Ventral view of lizard mite dermatitis.

What's Wrong With My Iguana?   39

PROTRUSIONS, FRONT AND BACK

Any structure protruding from the vent should be considered a medical emergency. Possible structures involved include the colon, bladder, hemipenis, or cloaca itself. Keep the structure moist using eyewash solution or water, and get your iguana to a veterinarian immediately.

A veterinarian will sedate the iguana and attempt to replace the structure, as well as determine the cause of the prolapse. Inability to replace and maintain a structure in its proper location will require additional surgery. **IN ANY CASE, THE LONGER YOU WAIT, THE MORE DIFFICULT THE PROBLEM BECOMES TO CORRECT, AND THE LOWER THE CHANCES THE IGUANA HAS TO SURVIVE.**

If no veterinary help is available immediately, you may be able to shrink the structure by using sugar water (add sugar to warm water until you have a concentrated solution i.e. no more sugar dissolves). Repeatedly apply the sugar water (syrup also works) to the protruding structure and try to use a blunt, smooth object to attempt to push the structure back in. Once in place, you must consider placing a pressure bandage on the vent area. Leave the bandage in place no longer than one to two days however, or until iguana is seen by a veterinarian. Even if you have successfully replaced the protrusion, you should still seek professional veterinary advice and treatment.

Sometimes something very serious is causing the problem. Swollen, enlarged kidneys may be responsible for a prolapsed colon or cloaca, and this demonstrates the need for professional evaluation. Indeed, if the underlying problem is not diagnosed and corrected, the prolapse may reoccur.

Occasionally, one or two hard objects may protrude from the vent which appear waxy or gelatinous in nature. If the lizard is a male, these are likely to be sperm plugs. Sometimes they can be gently pulled out of the hemipenal sheath without sedation. Sometimes they can't. If you can't remove the entire plug, stop and let the veterinarian do it. If you break the sperm plug, it will be much more difficult to remove later. These plugs are perhaps the only non-emergency situation involving protrusions from the cloaca, although failure to remove them promptly may result in some discomfort and possibly a local infection.

Moving to the front end of the iguana, protrusion of the tongue is also possible. Typically, this occurs secondary to MBD. Remember that the tip of the tongue is normally brighter pink or red than the rest of the tongue. However, if it is constantly protruding, it may take on a dried out, dark red appearance. A topical moisturizing agent will be needed to protect the tongue tip. KY Jelly® has been used with good results, although some cases may require a topical antibiotic. Silvadine Cream® applied sparingly to the tongue tip has worked extremely well.

Remember however, that any topical treatment is only palliative (not solving the underlying problem), and treatment of the underlying MBD is critical to completely and permanently resolving the protruding tongue.

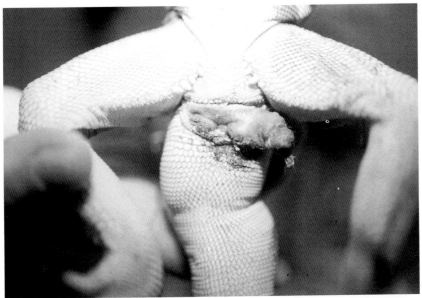

Protrusion from the vent. Almost all cases of protrusion from the vent are serious and require veterinary care. In this case, one hemipenis is protruding secondary to nerve damage from scoliosis (note the crooked tail).

RESPIRATORY PROBLEMS

Respiratory infections in iguanas are very rare. However, iguanas commonly sneeze. This is normal behavior for iguanas that are excreting salt. In fact, the presence of white, flaky material around the nares (nostrils) or on the cage glass is salt they have excreted. In these situations, the nostrils are usually dry, and no bubbles are visible. Should the nostrils have a discharge, or if bubbles are present, or if there is any open mouth breathing, an infection is highly likely. Respiratory infections are characterized by location, with the term "upper" being used to refer to infections in the sinuses or nasal passages, and "lower" referring to infections involving the bronchi and lungs. Fluid in the lungs, or inflammation of the lungs is often referred to as pneumonia. Any respiratory infection, regardless of location, is a serious matter, and professional help should be sought immediately. In the meantime, warm up the lizard's cage. Additional heat may help your iguana fight off an infection.

An allergy can produce similar signs. This is suspected in cases of poor cage ventilation, the use of aromatic wood chips as a substrate (i.e. cedar), or chemical irritants such as cigarette smoke.

Examine and correct the environment first, before any other therapy. An antibiotic may be started immediately however, if the signs are severe, and there is suspicion of infection.

SCOLIOSIS (CURVATURE OF THE SPINE)

There are two main reasons for curvature of the spine in iguanas. The most common reason is chronic metabolic bone disease (MBD). A poor diet fed to young, rapidly growing iguanas may result in a severe curvature of the spine along with other deformities. See the section on MBD.

The second cause of scoliosis is chronic burning of the spinal musculature on one side. These muscles may die. Without any resistance, the healthy muscles on the other side slowly pull the spine into a curved position. Typically the owner is unaware that a burn is occurring or that the muscle on that side is being damaged. If you see a color change on one side only, your iguana may be getting burned by a radiant heat source (i.e. light or ceramic heat emitter). Check by measuring the temperature at the basking site after the heat source has been on for several hours. If a burn is suspected, see the section on *Burns*.

Unfortunately, there is little that can be done to correct this condition (scoliosis) once it occurs, regardless of the cause. Back braces have been tried, but have met with limited success, and most iguanas resist wearing them. In addition, the problem tends to be slowly progressive, worsening as the iguana ages.

As usual, the best cure is prevention. Offering a high quality diet and providing the proper lighting will prevent both of these causes of scoliosis. If you see a change in the color of an iguana on one side only, or the beginnings of curvature of the spine, see your veterinarian immediately. He/she may be able to arrest the process that is creating the problem.

Scoliosis. This iguana ate nothing but apples for many years. A balanced diet must be fed.

SEIZURES, TREMORS AND GENERALIZED WEAKNESS

U ncontrolled movement, often accompanied by muscle tremors, is termed a seizure. A seizure is actually very frightening to watch, and iguanas may literally flip on their backs or roll uncontrollably. They often appear demented, not responding to any environmental stimulus.

By far, the most common cause of seizures with muscle tremors is hypocalcemia (low levels of calcium in the blood, often associated with the adult form of metabolic bone disease). Other causes include hypoglycemia (low blood sugar), septicemia (bacteria in the bloodstream), toxemias (toxin in the bloodstream), encephalitis (inflammation of the brain), vitamin B_1 and E deficiencies, gout and possibly even epilepsy.

Treatment for seizures or tremors should immediately involve a reptile veterinarian. Blood should be collected and analyzed immediately in order to determine a treatment regime. In some cases, this may not be possible, and under such circumstances, the veterinarian will probably collect blood to sent off to a lab, and initiate treatment with injectable calcium, antibiotics and fluids. See the section on *Medicines* for the doses of Calphosan®, fluids and antibiotics.

SOFT BENDABLE BONES

When the bones of the lower jaw become easily deformable and pressure on the lower jaw actually causes the eyes to partially protrude, they are too soft. This is a classic sign of metabolic bone disease (MBD). Another classic sign is "floppy toes". Typically a healthy iguana has strong toes which grip the substrate (and owner's skin), and have recognizable bending places (i.e. the joints). In iguanas with advanced MBD, the toes become floppy and rubber-like. One is reminded of the large shoes of clowns, in which the heel is placed down first and the floppy front end (in this case the toes) follows. The toes can also be bent in any direction.

Upon observing these signs, one can be sure that MBD is present. There are no other causes for generalized softness of the bones, although there may be multiple causes for the MBD. The treatment for this disease is discussed in the section on MBD and in the summary of care in captivity. Be prepared to handle with care during this stage of the disease. **BONES THIS SOFT MAY BE EASILY DAMAGED AND BOTH THE SPINAL COLUMN AND THE SPINAL CORD ARE AT RISK OF INJURY!** Toes this soft cannot shed skin properly, and the retained skin can form constricting bands around them, which cuts off the circulation and may lead to loss of the toe tips. This is referred to by veterinarians as avascular necrosis.

MBD has far-reaching effects. There are many other sequelae to this devastating disease, aside from just soft bones. See the section on *Metabolic Bone Disease* for a more complete discussion.

Bendable fingers. Another classic sign of MBD

SWELLING (JAWS, ABDOMEN, TOES, LEGS, SKIN, EYES AND TAIL)

JAWS

Various body parts may become swollen for a number of different reasons. The lower jaw and the thighs are most commonly affected if metabolic bone disease is present. Bilaterally symmetrical (equal on both sides) swelling involving any bones should make one suspicious of metabolic bone disease.

ABDOMEN

Causes of abdominal swelling include tumors and infections but most commonly, bloating. Females with a snout vent length of greater than 9 1/2 inches (24 cm) may also be gravid (containing eggs).

In the case of abdominal bloating, gas build up secondary to a blockage is possible but most commonly it is associated with poor passage of ingested material, often related to poor gut muscle tone following metabolic bone disease. Oral children's simethicone solutions such as Gas-X® may be administered orally at a dose of 1-10 drops to help relieve the bloating but a veterinarian should be consulted to administer an enema and relieve the blockage (if blockage is present). Torsion of the cecum will also cause bloating and this is a surgical emergency which can require radiographs in order to diagnose.

TOES

Swellings of the toes (or joints in the toes) may be caused by fractures, infection or gout. Radiographs may be taken in order to distinguish which problem is occurring, and determine treatment. Wire cages and very abrasive substrates may predispose to fractures or infections respectively. Iguanas with soft bones (MBD) and long claws that are housed on newspaper tend to develop fractured toes or twisted toes. Trim the nails and provide them with a substrate where they can use their claws such as Astroturf. Then correct the underlying metabolic bone disease by improving the quality of the diet and lighting. Of course, multiple toe fractures may be managed by splinting. The most effective technique has been to use a cotton ball to wrap the toes

Bent and broken claws. This usually happens when an iguana is housed in certain wire cages, or on abrasive substrates. Sometimes severe bending occurs when the substrate is very flat, like newspaper, because the claws have nothing to dig in, and become chronically twisted to one side. Rebreaking and setting the claws straight under anesthesia has proven successful in some cases.

around, and then wrapping the foot with a non-stick wrap, such as Vet-Wrap®.

Gout is the deposition of uric acid in body tissues. When it occurs in the toes of feet, it results in obvious swelling. Blood work <u>may</u> reveal an elevated uric acid level, which supports the presence of this disease and suggests a treatment regime. Remove any animal protein sources from the diet. Your veterinarian may also recommend a drug called allopurinol at a dose of 5-10 mg/kg once per day.

LEGS

Swollen legs are almost always due to **FIBROUS OSTEODYSTROPHY**, one manifestation of metabolic bone disease about anywhere. Severe, prolonged swelling may result in necrotic (rotten tissue) areas in these bones, which is almost impossible to treat, so prompt, aggressive therapy is warranted before this occurs. I aggressively treat this disease with injectable vitamin D3, calcium and calcitonin, a hormone which puts calcium back in the bones rapidly.

Swollen thighs. This sign demonstrates fibrous osteodystrophy, another serious and classic manifestation of MBD.

As mentioned above, failure to rapidly reverse swollen thighs may result in circulatory compromise, tissue damage and infection. Ultimately, a badly affected leg may be impossible to save, so see your veterinarian immediately.

A swollen leg that is shorter than the opposite limb is usually fractured. Again, see your veterinarian.

SKIN

Swellings in the skin are usually abscesses (or pus pockets), but may be cysts, blisters or tumors. Small abscesses may be nicked with a razor and pus may be expressed. The wound may then be flushed with Betadine® solution (diluted 1/4 with water). Most of these are best treated by a veterinarian who may sedate the iguana in order to do a more thorough job of emptying and flushing the wound, or surgically remove the mass if it is a tumor. Cleaned abscesses may then be packed with Silvadine Cream® or Betadine Ointment® daily. Sometimes systemic (injectable) antibiotics may be necessary. I always advise injectable antibiotics because the bacteria in the abscess may have spread via the bloodstream. Ideally, the antibiotic or antibiotics chosen should be based upon a culture and sensitivity. **Remember, the**

abscess that you see may be accompanied by abscesses that you can't see! Hence, skin abscesses may be more serious and widespread than they look.

EYES

Swollen eyes in iguanas may be associated with post-ocular abscesses (abscesses behind the eye), hemorrhage or swollen blood vessels behind the eyes (which may be due to rough handling or stress) or MBD. Abscesses may occur anywhere and the presence of swollen eyes in an iguana that has abscesses elsewhere should make one suspicious of this.

A more severe eye infection.

Rough handling or heavy restraint may result in swollen eyes via swollen blood vessels, but this is usually rapidly reversible.

In the case of MBD, the skull may actually be too small for the eyes i.e. the skull may not have grown while the eyes have.

In all cases of eye swelling, have the lizard examined by a veterinarian as soon as possible.

TAIL

If the base of the tail is swollen, it is almost always due to MBD, specifically fibrous osteodystrophy, the same process that causes swelling of the back legs. Correct the diet and lighting, and see the section on MBD in this book.

Bilateral swellings on the ventral surface of the tail at its base are usually hemipenal bulges, and are normal for adult and sub-adult males. If there is any protrusion from the cloaca, or if there is asymmetrical swelling, contact a veterinarian immediately. This is also advisable if there is any redness associated with the area.

TRAUMA

Most cases of trauma in iguanas occur when they are out of their cages. They usually involve other pets, or accidents such as falling, or having something fall on them. Hence, the best way to prevent trauma is to house iguanas properly and prevent escapes. See specific headings for various traumatic problems.

Scratch trauma. The black spots here are from the needle sharp claws of other iguanas housed in a crowded cage.

VOMITING

While vomiting* is a rare problem in iguanas, it usually suggests a serious problem when it occurs. Causes of vomiting include: ingestion or exposure to a toxin, ingestion of a foreign body, or intestinal blockage. In any case, a veterinarian should be consulted. **AN IGUANA THAT IS VOMITING IS IN CRITICAL CONDITION AND THERE IS LITTLE THAT YOU CAN DO TO HELP YOUR PET WITHOUT PROFESSIONAL HELP.** A radiograph (X-ray) may reveal the cause of the problem and allow potentially lifesaving treatment. Keep in mind that the longer you wait, the worse the chances are to help your iguana.

One of the common and more rewarding cases of vomiting is when an iguana gets hair caught in the throat. This is usually associated with increased mucus in the mouth and throat, and careful examination may reveal a long hair wrapped around the glottis and trailing down into the stomach. Once the hair is removed, the iguana will rapidly improve.

NOTE:
*Regurgitation and vomiting cannot be easily distinguished in reptiles, so the term vomiting will be used here for any return of food or anything else to the mouth from the esophagus or the stomach.

SPECIAL TOPICS

BEHAVIOR

The behavior of iguanas is actually very complex, and perhaps could alone become the topic of an entire book. Many of the behaviors observed in captive iguanas, even captive hatchlings, have also been observed in wild iguanas. This would suggest that many of their behaviors are innate (or instinctual), rather than learned, even though the environmental stimuli may be very different. Undoubtedly, a great deal of their behavior in captivity is learned, and their experiences (good or bad) around people, may be the primary or major determining factor in how well they respond to people and indeed, how well they may adjust to captivity in general. This chapter will briefly discuss some of the behaviors as they may relate to medical problems. It is by no means meant to be a comprehensive review of all iguana behaviors.

ANOREXIA
Failure to eat is discussed in its own section. Remember that this may be stress-related or a psychological problem rather than a medical one. However, an anorexic iguana should be examined by your reptile veterinarian, who may need to perform several tests in order to determine if a medical or psychological problem exists.

AGITATION (OR IRRITABILITY)
Many things can make an iguana become irritable. Some iguanas become irritable prior to shedding, others never do. Abdominal pain, an injury, hunger, sexual readiness, territoriality, imminent egg-laying, the presence of a skin infection, external parasites such as mites, or even excessive restraint are some of the things that can cause an iguana to become irritable or agitated. Changes in color and aggressive postures are usually observed. Like cats, agitated iguanas may flick their tails from side to side very rapidly.

INAPPROPRIATE DEFECATION
Defecation at socially unacceptable times or places may occur with an iguana whose routine is disturbed, or just plain scared. Sometimes confining an iguana to a small area or cage induces defecation. Being handled by a stranger may induce defecation. Like cats however, it now appears that some iguanas may defecate in order to gain attention or to protest a change or a punishment.

HEAD BOBBING
Head bobbing is a territorial display. The intensity, as determined by the depth and the speed of the bobbing is an indication of just how territorial the iguana is. Very intense head bobbing may be associated with the lizard biting someone who approaches too closely.

HIDING

Hiding is a sign of maximum stress. Prolonged hiding may be associated with multiple system shutdown, including the gastrointestinal system and the immune system. Excessive disturbance of the lizard by the keeper, other people or another cage mate are the most likely causes. If there is no history of excessive disturbance by the keeper, and there are no other lizards in the same cage (or within sight!), then the environment itself should be considered unacceptable. Some iguanas may never adjust to captivity, regardless of how good the captive environment appears to us. These animals should be examined by a veterinarian to rule out medical problems, prior to concluding that they cannot adapt to captivity. Before doing anything drastic, you may want to consider allowing a friend to try keeping the iguana for a while.

INGESTION OF FOREIGN OBJECTS

The ingestion of unusual objects is referred to as *pica* by veterinarians. In mammals and other reptiles, it is believed to occur most commonly when an animal feels that there is a deficiency (of some mineral or vitamin) in the diet. Hence, an iguana suffering from MBD, or even a normal gravid iguana, may crave calcium and will ingest a variety of things in order to obtain that calcium. This can include gravel, plastic or metal screws and nails, rubber bands, or any object small enough to swallow. Ingestion of hard objects such as stones by other reptiles and birds (and even dinosaurs) is (or was) also thought to help aid with the mechanical digestion of food in animals that do not or can not chew their food before swallowing. Alligators and crocodiles are known to have a "gizzard" like structure where stones may aid in the breakdown of food. Iguanas do not possess a specialized thickened area for such materials in their stomachs, however, this process may actually occur to some extent in their large stomachs. Nevertheless, the presence of gravel or other hard, small objects in the cage is not advisable since they are not considered a necessity, and are more likely to cause an intestinal obstruction than aid in digestion.

There may be other reasons for this behavior, but any time it is observed, a visit to the veterinarian is in order. Firstly, it will be necessary to determine how much foreign material has been ingested by taking a radiograph (X-ray) and secondly, to determine if a deficiency of calcium is indeed the cause.

OPENING OF THE MOUTH

Firstly, iguanas do yawn occasionally and this is not a problem. Basically, it appears very similar to what we might expect in a mammal. An open mouth associated with rapid breathing is **panting**. It is believed that panting, as in some mammals, allows an iguana to cool off slightly when its body temperature is very high. This occurs even when they can move to a cooler temperature, so they may use this behavior to "fine tune" to very high preferred temperatures, and thereby can remain at those high temperatures for a longer time. This is an innate behavior. I have observed it in three-day old hatchlings.

Sometimes however, open mouth-breathing can suggest a respiratory infection or abdominal pain.

Lastly, an open mouth in an iguana showing an aggressive posture (i.e. raised whole body stance with one side presented) means only one thing. The iguana is ready to bite. Heed this warning!

ZONING OUT

"Zoning out" is a rather recent expression used to describe people that seem oblivious to their surroundings. It is also used widely to describe a similar situation in the green iguana. Some iguanas, when stressed due to physical restraint or a major traumatic event, appear to enter a trance. If severely stressed they may go into shock and die. The actual hormonal/chemical changes are unknown.

PHOBIAS

Fear is either an instinctive or learned behavior of avoidance. Natural or innate fears of iguana seem to include birds, large mammals (including cats and dogs), snakes and other large reptiles (including larger iguanas), open spaces with no cover, and for many iguanas, standing water. As with other animals, innate fears can either be overcome or intensified. Fear of other things (like veterinarians) can be learned. Living in constant fear results in stress, which can lead to illness.

FIRST AID

An iguana that is severely depressed, dehydrated or bleeding requires emergency care. These "first" treatments are referred to as first aid, and they are briefly outlined here: 1) Hemostasis (stopping bleeding) 2) Rehydration 3) Warmth 4) Nutritional Support.

Once an iguana is stabilized by addressing the first three concerns above (i.e. there is no bleeding, and the patient is warm and well hydrated), nutritional support is the next concern. This has been addressed by assist-feeding many liquid or semi-liquid diets over the years. These diets have included various baby foods, dog foods and veterinary products. Recently, veterinarians have been recommending a readily available human nutritional supplement called Ensure®. The regular (as opposed to high-protein) Ensure® is wonderfully suited for tube-feeding iguanas, and the strawberry-flavored variety appears to be well accepted. Some veterinarians add a banana to the liquid and blend it in. This liquid or others can be given at a dose of 1-3 ml per hundred grams of body weight, either daily in the case of 1 ml per hundred grams, or on alternate days, in the case of 2-3 ml per 100 grams, until feeding resumes.

Warmth may be provided via a hot/warm water bottle, a heating pad turned to low and watched carefully, or a radiant heat source. Be careful not to allow burning.

RECOGNIZING SHOCK
As in mammals, acute blood loss or severe trauma may result in shock-type of situation, where the circulatory system is compromised. A pale, "mustard yellow" skin color in a collapsing iguana, is suggestive of shock! This is a medical emergency, so follow the procedure above, but seek professional veterinary care immediately.

---

1) Bleeding. Apply pressure to bleeding area, and see the section on _Bleeding._

2) Dehydration. Administer oral fluids and see the section on _Dehydration._

3) Cold exposure. Provide gentle heat and see the section on _Cold Exposure_.

4) Starvation. Assist feed or tube feed only after correcting dehydration.

PROBLEM/SOLUTION CHART

PROBLEM	PROBABLE CAUSE	SOLUTION
POOR APPETITE/ANOREXIA	1. Stress from move 2. Other iguanas 3. Infection 4. Metabolic problem 5. Gravid female 6. Intestinal blockage 7. Intestinal parasites 8. Tumor	1. Stable environment 2. Separate 3. See vet 4. See vet 5. Provide egg laying site 6. See vet 7. See vet 8. See vet
BUMPS, LUMPS	1. Bite wounds 2. Cage too moist or too cool or too dirty 3. Burns	1. Separate 2. Warm, dry, clean cage, check ventilation 3. Check heat source and see vet
CONSTIPATION	1. Hugging ventral heat source 2. Humidity too low 3. Not enough dietary fiber 4. Lack of exercise 5. Overfeeding 6. Kidney disease 7. All causes	1. Provide heat from above 2. increase humidity 3. Increase fiber 4. Increase cage size 5. Feed less 6. Fluids, see vet 7. Warm watersoaks laxatives, enema
DIARRHEA	1. Bacterial or parasitic infection 2. Dietary indiscretion or temp. too low 3. Excessive fruit or water intake	1. Deworm or see vet 2. Kaopectate® or no food 3. Reduce fruit intake
DYSECDYSIS/ IMPROPER SHED	1. Malnourishment 2. Humidity too low 3. Lizard mites 4. Injuries 5. Skin infection	1. Improve nutrition 2. Increase humidity 3. Eliminate mites 4. Assist shed 5. Treat infection, assist shedding
FAILURE TO LAY EGGS	1. Not gravid 2. Egg bound 3. MBD 4. Eggs resorbed.	1. Wait or see vet 2. See vet 3. See vet 4. Feed more, reduce stress, parasite check.

PROBLEM	PROBABLE CAUSE	SOLUTION
OPEN MOUTH BREATHING/SNEEZING	1. Panting (normal) 2. Respiratory infection 3. Allergic reaction	1. Check heats ource 2. See vet 3. Move to fresh air, change substrate
STOMATITIS	1. Foods too sweet/mushy 2. Gums exposed/MBD 3. Trauma to mouth	1. Improve diet 2. See vet 3. Topical anibiotic
VOMITING	1. Foreign body 2. Intestinal blockage 3. Toxicity 4. Kidney failure	1. See vet 2. See vet 3. See vet 4. See vet
NOSE TRAUMA (ROSTRAL ABRASION)	1. Small cage with clear sides	1. Larger cage with visual barriers
BLOATING	1. MBD 2. Spinal injury 3. Partial blockage 4. All causes	1. See vet 2. See vet 3. Laxative, enema, see vet 4. Simethicone
HEAD TILT	1. Trauma to head 2. Middle ear infection	1. See vet 2. See vet
DARK SPOTS	1. Scratches from other iguanas 2. Bacterial or fungal infection 3. Stress	1. Separate 2. Topical antibiotic/antifungal see vet 3. Reduce stress
COLOR CHANGE	1. Yellow/shock 2. Black/pain 3. Orange/breeding	1. See vet 2. See vet 3. Reduce daily amt. of light
PROTRUSION	1. Prolapsed colon, hemipenis, tongue	1. See vet
SWELLING	1. Multiple causes	1. See test and see vet
TREMORS	1. MBD 2. Toxicity 3. Septicemia	1. See vet 2. See vet 3. See vet

GOUT AND CALCIFICATION OF SOFT TISSUE

These two disorders are discussed together because they are common disorders of excess. Neither is easily diagnosed without radiographs and blood work, and both have vague signs which can be seen with many diseases. These include anorexia and lethargy, and sometimes muscle tremors or seizures.

GOUT

Gout is the deposition of uric acid in either joint spaces or soft tissue structures. In the first case, it is called articular gout, and may result in swollen toes or feet. In the later case, there are uric acid granules distributed widely throughout the kidneys. Liver, lungs and heart, or all of the above may be affected. This is called visceral gout. There are several possible causes of gout, but the most frequently suspected cause is excessive animal protein in the diet. These proteins are high in certain kinds of chemicals, which contribute to the formation of uric acid, and thereby its deposition. Other causes of gout include a chronic lack of drinking water, and excessive use of nephrotoxic (kidney damaging) antibiotics. One of the most potentially nephrotoxic groups of antibiotics are the aminoglycosides, a group containing such effective antibiotics as neomycin, kanamycin, gentocin, and amikacin. The latter is

Swollen toes. The three most likely causes are fractures, infections or gout. In this case, bite-wound trauma resulted in infection.

one of the most commonly used antibiotics in iguanas today. Indeed, amikacin sulfate appears to be a safe and effective drug when used at the proper dosage. Certainly, it is even safer when administered along with injectable fluids i.e. sterile electrolyte solutions are administered in the abdominal cavity (intraperitoneally) at a dose of 10 ml/kg per day during the course of amikacin. However, these drugs, including amikacin, should never be used in an iguana that may be suffering from kidney disease, dehydration, or gout. Instead, a non-nephrotoxic antibiotic should be chosen. This would include most of the cephalosporins. See the section on *Medicines* for the appropriate dose of amikacin and other antibiotics.

Regardless of the cause, gout is a serious disorder, which requires dietary change, increased water availability, and possibly a medication called allopurinol. See the section on swelling (under toes) and medicines.

CALCIFICATION OF SOFT TISSUES
If excess calcium or vitamin D containing products (i.e. dog food, cat food) are ingested by a iguana over a prolonged period, signs of hypervitaminosis D may be observed. The most significant feature of this disease is the calcification of soft tissues. These include arteries and veins, as well as the intestines, and other major organs. In advanced cases, the major blood vessels are outlined by calcium and readily visible radiographically, and the calcium level in the blood may be two to four times the normal level.

Treatment involves correcting the diet to eliminate sources of excess calcium or vitamin D, increasing the water intake (and giving injectable fluids as discussed above), and if possible, using a drug called calcitonin. Calcitonin is a hormone that puts calcium back in the bone and takes it out of the bloodstream. See the section on *Medicines* for the dose. Remember that the drug must be given for several weeks past the point that the blood level of calcium has returned to normal.

In summary, both of these disease conditions appear to be preventable, but once they occur, professional help may be necessary to help give your iguana a fighting chance.

MEDICINES AND MEDICATING

Medicating iguanas is not very difficult most of the time. Oral medications may be administered by gently pulling down on the dewlap while holding the sides of the upper jaw with the opposite hand. A good-tasting medication like Neocalglucon® or Reptilaid® may usually be delivered into the mouth and will be voluntarily swallowed. A less tasteful medication may be refused and sometimes needs to be delivered farther down in the throat. A regular syringe or eye dropper may be used for this purpose. For sure delivery into the stomach, a soft rubber tube may be used.

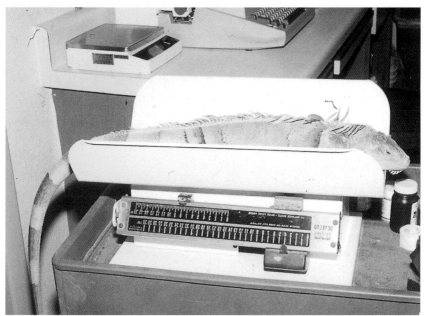

A green iguana must be weighed to determine accurate dosage of medication.

Topical medications should be applied once daily. Bandaging may be helpful in some cases, and can usually be accomplished extremely well with non-stick bandaging material such as Vet-Wrap®.

A number of sprays are useful in treating iguanas. Protectants such as NuSkin® have been very helpful in protecting wounds and increasing the rate of healing in other reptiles and have worked well on iguanas.

Injectable medications are usually delivered by small gauge needles (22, 23, 25, 27 gauge) either intramuscularly (IM) or subcutaneously (SC) in iguanas. Most antibiotics and vitamins are injected IM, while most sterile fluids are injected SC or intraperitoneally (IP) (in the abdominal cavity).

Since reptiles have a renal-portal circulatory pathway (which basically means that the blood in the back half of the body goes to the kidneys first), it is usually recommended that antibiotic injections be given in the front half. The most common location is the triceps muscle. Some antibiotics do not seem affected by this system, but it is standard practice now anyway. Most vitamin injections are also given IM and a good location for these are in the base of the tail in the thick muscle along the top. Be careful however, because occasionally a stinging substance injected there will cause an iguana to drop its tail.

Subcutaneous injections can be given along almost anywhere but usually are easier to give along the side.

MEDICINES

Several tables of antibiotics, and anti-parasitic agents are presented in this section. Remember that new research often indicates changes in drug doses, so check with your veterinarian and follow their advice. There is no substitute for a good physical exam, diagnostic testing and accurate weight to determine the proper treatment regime. Antibiotics may or not be indicated for a particular problem.

Subcutaneous calcium injection.

MOST COMMONLY USED DRUGS IN IGUANAS

PROBLEM	DRUG	DOSE
BACTERIAL INFECTION	AMIKACIN 50 mg/ml ENROFLOXACIN 23 mg/ml CHLORAMPHENICOL CEFTAZIDIME CARBENICILLIN TRIMETHOPRIM SULFA CIPROFLOXACIN PIPERACILLIN	2.5 mg/kg every 72 hours IM (0.0227ml/lb)# 5 mg/kg every 24 hours IM initially then PO 50 mg/kg SC SID 20 mg/kg IM every 72 hours 400 mg/kg IM every 72 hours 30 mg/kg PO every 48 hours 10 mg/kg PO every 48 hours 50 mg/kg IM every 72 hours
INTESTINAL PARASITISM		
Amoebiasis	METRONIDAZOLE (FLAGYL®)	60-125 mg/kg*PO+
Coccidiosis	SULFADIMETHOXINE	90 mg/kg 1st day PO then 45 mg/kg for 4 days in a row
Nematodes (hooks, whips, rounds)	IVERMECTIN 15 mg/ml FENBENDAZOLE 100 mg/ml	0.02 ml/kg(0.01ml/b)+ 50-100 mg/kg+ (.23-.46 mg/lb)
Cestodes and Trematodes (tapes and flukes)	PRAZIQUANTEL 56.8 mg/ml	7.5-30 mg/kg+(3-14 mg/lb)
EXTERNAL PARASITISM		
Acariasis (mites and ticks)	IVERMECTIN 10 mg/ml	0.01 ml/lb PO or SC or IM+ Can also dilute 1/2 cc in 1 L (quart) of water and spray every 2 or 3 days for 3 weeks.
	5% SEVIN DUST	Dust cage for 2-24 hours.

KEY TO SYMBOLS
#3-5 treatments usually
+= Repeat in two weeks
PO = By Mouth
IM = Intramuscular Injection
SC = Subcutaneous Injection
SID = Once per day

IGUANA ANTIBIOTIC CHART I

AMIKACIN SULFATE 50MG/ML

WEIGHT (GRAMS/POUNDS)	DILUTION	DOSE (ML)#
5 g	1/100	0.025+
10 g (0.02 lbs)	1/100	0.050
15 g (0.03 lbs)	1/100	0.075
20 g(0.05 lbs)	1/10	0.010
30 g(0.07 lbs)	1/10	0.015
40 g(0.09 lbs)	1/10	0.020
50 g(0.11 lbs)	1/10	0.025
100 g(0.22 lbs)	1/10	0.050
200 g(0.44 lbs)	None	0.010
300 g(0.66 lbs)	None	0.015
400 g(0.88 lbs)	None	0.020
500 g(1.1 lbs)	None	0.025
600 g(1.3 lbs)	None	0.030
700 g(1.5 lbs)	None	0.035
800 g(1.8 lbs)	None	0.040
900 g(2.0 lbs)	None	0.045
1000 g(2.2 lbs)	None	0.050
1200 g(2.6 lbs)	None	0.060
1500 g(3.3 lbs)	None	0.075
1800 g(3.9 lbs)	None	0.090
2000 g(4.4 lbs)	None	0.100
2300 g(5.0 lbs)	None	0.115

#Recommended dose from literature is 2.5 mg/kg given IM every 72 hours. A loading dose (first dose) of 5.0 mg/kg is also recommended.

+ We have calculated doses one digit beyond the accuracy of the common smallest syringes (0.5 and 1.0 syringes). Round off to the nearest one hundredth of a cc.

IGUANA ANTIBIOTIC CHART II

BAYTRIL (ENROFLOXACIN) 23MG/ML

WEIGHT (GRAMS/POUNDS)	DILUTION	DOSE (ML)#
5 g	1/10	0.01
10 g(0.02 lbs)	1/10	0.02
15 g(0.03 lbs)	1/10	0.03
20 g(0.05 lbs)	1/10	0.04
30 g(0.07 lbs)	1/10	0.06
40 g(0.09 lbs)	1/10	0.09
50 g(0.11 lbs)	None	0.01
100 g(0.22 lbs)	None	0.02
150 g(0.33 lbs)	None	0.03
200 g(0.44 lbs)	None	0.04
250 g(0.55 lbs)	None	0.05
300 g(0.66 lbs)	None	0.06
350 g(0.77 lbs)	None	0.08
400 g(0.88 lbs)	None	0.09
450 g(0.99 lbs)	None	0.10
500 g(1.1 lbs)	None	0.11
600 g(1.3 lbs)	None	0.13
700 g(1.5 lbs)	None	0.15
800 g(1.8 lbs)	None	0.17
900 g(2.0 lbs)	None	0.20
1000 g(2.2 lbs)	None	0.22
1500 g(3.3 lbs)	None	0.33
2000 g(4.4 lbs)	None	0.44

#Recommended dose from literature is 5 mg/kg given IM initially then PO every 24 hours. A loading dose (first dose) of 5.0-10 mg/kg is also recommended.

IM = Intramuscular injection.

METABOLIC BONE DISEASE
THE HARD FACTS

In spite of scores of articles and books on how to keep iguanas healthy in captivity, malnourishment resulting in severe metabolic bone disease is still the most common and devastating disease of captive iguanas. It has many different manifestations and sequelae, and appears to be at the root of over 90% of all medical problems that iguanas develop. For example, appetite loss, bleeding, constipation, exposure gingivitis, stomatitis (mouth infection), dystocia (egg-binding), failure to grow, fractures, paralysis, paresis (weakness), tongue and cloacal protrusions, scoliosis (curvature of the spine), seizures, tremors, and swellings of the jaws, legs, eyes, abdomen, and tail, may all be directly or indirectly related to metabolic bone disease. Thus, one always needs to be suspicious of MBD when just about any problem is encountered. Many of my clients are shocked to learn that their iguana is afflicted with this disease when they bring it in for something unrelated (or is it?).

What exactly is MBD? Basically, MBD is the removal of calcium from the bone in order to maintain the calcium level elsewhere. Calcium serves many functions, and is important in blood clotting, heart, gut, and voluntary muscle function.

Axillary (armpit) dermatitis. An infection in the armpit of this iguana may require removal of skin trapped in this area.

So MBD doesn't just affect the bones. If it does, it usually is more obvious in young iguanas or females about to lay eggs. In fact, some authors consider that there are two basic manifestations of MBD, namely adult MBD and juvenile MBD. Juvenile MBD may be recognized by the soft, pliable bones of the jaws, swollen thighs, and a poor growth rate. Adult MBD is usually manifested by muscle tremors secondary to hypocalcemia (low blood levels of calcium).

Treatment usually depends upon correcting the diet to include more greens (collards, turnip greens, mustard greens, and kale among others) and less of the low calcium vegetables like squash, broccoli flowers, and fruits. It also depends upon improving the UV lighting, which **<u>MUST</u>** include some time out in natural sunlight, as well as the appropriate UV-B bulbs inside. See the section on *Soft Bendable Bones* for a discussion on types of lights.

Acute signs may be aided by injections of calcium, Vitamin D3, and possibly calcitonin. This should be determined by your veterinarian. Administering calcitonin to an iguana with low blood levels of calcium could be fatal, so it is best used cautiously. See the section on *Medicines* for doses.

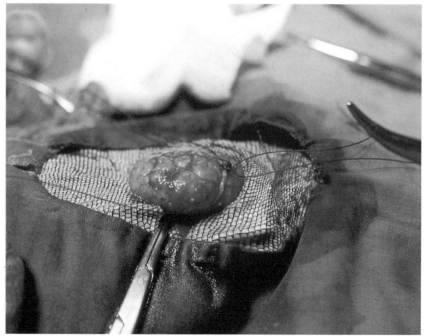

Surgery reveals a swollen kidney.

PERSONAL HYGIENE AND QUARANTINE

Iguanas are capable of carrying potential human pathogens without showing any signs at all. Examples include many bacteria such as *Salmonella, Campylobacter* and *Clostridium* species. As apparently healthy carriers, they can be particularly dangerous when personal hygiene or quarantine are not practiced. Families with immunocompromised individuals, particularly young children and older individuals, should consider not keeping iguanas or other reptiles for this reason. It should be noted however that the risk of acquiring a disease from a reptile is substantially reduced by following common sense hygienic procedures. In addition, any other animals in the house including iguanas, will be protected by establishing a quarantine system. This involves maintaining a new reptile in a separate area for 1-3 months. Once they have remained healthy throughout the quarantine period, they may be introduced into the same room housing other pet reptiles.

Common sense hygiene includes: 1) Washing hands every time an iguana is handled, especially prior to eating anything or smoking. 2) Not kissing your iguana. 3) Not cleaning iguana food dishes or water bowls in the kitchen sink.

If there is any question regarding *Salmonella*, a culture and sensitivity test may be performed on a fresh fecal sample of the iguana in question. A positive culture indicates that the iguana is shedding the organism. However, a positive culture now may be negative in one to six months, while a negative culture now, could be positive in 1 to 6 months. Thus, there is a potential risk involved, and those families maintaining iguanas must take some common sense precautions. To put it in perspective however, one has a much greater chance of contracting *Salmonella* from poorly cooked poultry than from a pet iguana. Don't forget, iguana bites may also introduce some nasty bacteria into their human keepers. Clean such wounds thoroughly and consult your doctor. I have cultured *Clostridium tetani* from the mouth of an iguana. This is the organism that causes tetanus! Admittedly, this is a rare finding in my experience. Nevertheless, it points out that there is a risk in dealing with these animals. So enjoy them, but wash those hands and use common sense.

PREVENTIVE MEDICINE

As mentioned elsewhere in this book, iguanas can live 20 or more years. Many die unexpectedly under 10 years of age however. In this section, we will discuss the leading causes of death in young iguanas, and talk about how to avoid them.

KIDNEY DISEASE

Rapidly emerging as one of the most common, if not the most common disease in iguanas older than 3 years of age, kidney disease is almost always fatal within a year of diagnosis. The signs are nebulous and non-specific. The affected animal may be lethargic, anorexic and dehydrated. In advanced cases, it may be constipated since the enlarged kidneys may impinge upon the colon and block the passage of stool. The history may make a veterinarian suspicious, but only blood work and radiographs can confirm the diseases exist. Treatment involves fluids and phosphate binding agents such as Amphogel® plus dietary correction and natural sunlight. One may also increase fluid intake by soaking or spraying vegetables prior to feeding them. The cause of this disease is not completely understood, so prevention is problematic. It is highly suspected that animal protein sources such as dog food, cat food, monkey biscuits and trout chow may contribute to the onset of this problem, so these foods should be avoided.

METABOLIC BONE DISEASE

The classic and perhaps still the most common disease of iguanas, this disease or its sequelae probably kills hundreds of thousands of iguanas annually. Juvenile MBD may be recognized by the soft, pliable bones of the jaws, swollen thighs and poor growth rate. Adult MBD is usually

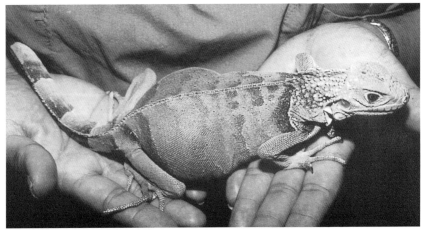

Bloating is often seen several weeks to years after metabolic bone disease or a fractured back.

manifested by muscle tremors secondary to hypocalcemia. Both can be fatal, or lead to situations which become progressively worse.

The cause is usually dietary, or due to insufficient UV light, but it may be associated with kidney failure. See the sections on *Soft, Bendable Bones, Metabolic Bone Disease* and *Brief Summary of Care in Captivity*. Feed more greens (collards, turnip greens mustard greens and kale among others) and less of low calcium vegetables like squash, broccoli flowers and fruits. Provide the proper lighting. Allow your veterinarian to perform complete blood chemistries once every two years in order to detect evidence of metabolic bone disease and other potential problems. Annual physical exams are also advisable.

INFECTIONS
Scratches, bites and other traumatic injuries, if left untreated may become infected. Infection spreads rapidly in small, stressed (immunocompromised) animals, and may result in death within days or weeks.

House singly and treat wounds immediately with topical antibiotics. Consider a visit to the veterinarian, and possible injectable antibiotics if the wounds appear more serious. If a veterinarian suspects that an infection has spread to the bone, he/she may wish to take radiographs (X-rays) to confirm the infection, and then prescribe long term antibiotics (3 to 6 weeks). Correct the environment promptly.

Infections involving the mouth are also very common. See the section on *Dental Disease* in this book for a discussion on how to interpret and treat these problems.

Ringworm (skin fungus) infection on the side of an iguana.

Of course, one of the most common manifestations of infections in iguanas are abscesses or granulomas. These sometimes huge lumps need to be surgically removed, and then the patient placed on injectable antibiotics. Also see the section on *Lumps and Bumps*.

UNTREATED PARASITISM

As mentioned elsewhere, untreated pinworms are capable of causing serious gastrointestinal signs, possibly leading to the death of many young iguanas. Routine deworming and fecal exams will help to eliminate this as a major cause of death in young iguanas.

FOREIGN BODY (SUBSTRATE) INGESTION

In spite of numerous warnings, many people still use wood chips for juvenile iguanas. While it is attractive, it is an accident waiting to happen. Ingestion of the substrate and the resulting blockage is still a major cause of death in young iguanas. This is another completely preventable problem. Unfortunately, once it occurs, it is usually diagnosed too late to save the iguana.

In summary, the top five killers of young iguanas are all preventable through proper husbandry techniques and diet. In addition, all of these diseases can be treated successfully if diagnosed early enough. Therefore, a regular (annual) physical is strongly recommended, along with fecal exams and occasional blood work. Perhaps most iguanas can survive to thirty or more years of age with improved care.

SPAYING AND NEUTERING

Iguanas are now commonly being spayed or neutered for medical or behavioral problems.

Young female iguanas with MBD (even mild MBD) are prime candidates for dystocia (egg-binding). If they cannot finish laying their eggs, they will die. Surgery to remove the eggs and perform an ovariohysterectomy at the same time is described in the section on dystocia.

Neutering males is usually done to reduce aggressive behavior, although its effectiveness is still questionable. Several veterinarians seem certain that it does reduce aggressive behavior, and the procedure is being performed regularly.

Remember that the cost of both of these procedures is justifiably high. Both anesthesia and surgery are time consuming in reptiles, and require special equipment and skill. At the time of this writing, spaying and neutering iguanas costs about twice as much as spaying or neutering a large dog, and requires more time than that procedure.

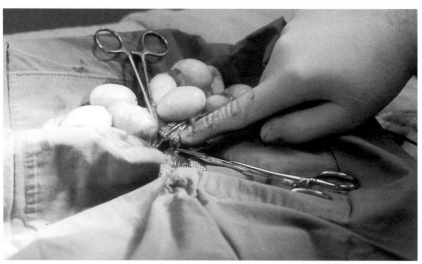

Spaying. This surgery may save an iguana's life and prevent the problem in the future.

TRANSPORTATION

Many people travel with their iguanas, and fortunately most iguanas travel fairly well. That is, they travel well once they adjust to their traveling cage, which becomes their home during the first week of travel. Prior to that adjustment (acclimation) they will rarely eat.

Food or lack thereof, is not the main threat to traveling iguanas however; excessive heat or cold is. Inside a <u>non-insulated</u> container, a few minutes in the hot sun is fatal. See the section on *Overheating*. Similarly, exposure to intense or prolonged cold can result in sudden death or a fatal respiratory infection. Thus, insulated carriers are advisable, whether they be fancy as complete habitats inside of mobile homes, or a Styrofoam® box. For short trips, one may place the iguana inside of a pillowcase, tie a knot and place the pillowcase inside of an insulated cooler. Igloo® boxes have worked very well. Some iguana keepers place crumpled newspaper inside of the bag (pillowcase) or box for added cushioning and security.

For longer trips, larger cages are advisable, and food and water should be provided. Even though they are un-insulated, plastic dog and cat carriers make excellent transport containers, and they come in all sizes. In fact, these cages have worked well for transporting iguanas on planes. Remember that most planes house traveling pets in air conditioned or heated areas, but there are times when a cage may sit in direct sunlight at the airport for 10 minutes or so. This is when an insulated container earns its keep. Check with the airline you are using for specific shipping directions. The author has found Delta Airlines to be the leader in the area of shipping reptiles at the time of this writing. They appear very experienced in shipping these animals, and rarely let them sit in a very hot or cold area for any length of time.

As with dogs and cats, tranquilizers are sometimes useful. Particularly nervous lizards may benefit from a low dose of oral Diazepam (1/4 to 1 mg/lb every 8 hours as needed). This drug is advantageous for two reasons. Firstly, it calms down iguanas and makes them less likely to traumatize their noses by running into things. Secondly, it often stimulates the appetite during times of change or stress. Happy traveling!

VETERINARIANS
WHY YOU NEED ONE AND HOW TO
CHOOSE ONE

In the last ten years, veterinarians have made huge strides in under standing, diagnosing and treating reptiles. These are now several major texts devoted entirely to reptile and amphibian medicine and surgery (Frye, 1991; Mader, 1996). There are also several books that deal specifically with iguanas and their husbandry (de Vosjoli, 1992, Frye, 1995). Those veterinarians who treat reptiles regularly have a great deal of experience helping them as well as a tremendous arsenal of drugs which are useful. Many reptiles, including iguanas, are long lived (15-25 years) if cared for properly, and veterinary care can help achieve that long life. Annual physical exams, as well as fecal exams to check for parasites, and blood work to check for signs of organ failure or infection, are all important. Many of my clients are shocked to find out that their "healthy" iguana has some evidence of kidney disease, liver disease, or even herpes virus infection. Some of these cases can be managed effectively if caught early enough, and these iguanas will have a chance to live longer, healthier lives.

The cost of treating reptiles is generally slightly higher than the cost of treating dogs and cats. The reason for this is that reptile exams and client education included are far more time consuming than most dog and cat exams. Additionally, diagnostic tests usually require additional equipment or skill, resulting in costs which must be passed on to the client. A good reptile veterinarian will spend hundreds to thousands of dollars per years on educational materials, books, and reptile medicine seminars in order to stay current. There is also additional cost incurred in purchasing medicines which are particularly useful in reptiles, as well as caging and heating systems for these animals.

Hence, it is somewhat expensive to have an iguana treated properly, but it is usually well worth it. Choose a veterinarian that has some experience with reptiles. Check with your zoo, museum, pet shops, and herpetological society, and find out who they recommend. Good reptile veterinarians usually have reptiles of their own, and rarely show fear when examining or handling reptiles.

Make sure to call for an appointment (i.e. it is not an emergency) and show up. Not treating another patient in anticipation of your arrival costs a good deal of valuable time.

If you don't have an experienced reptile veterinarian nearby, find one who will at least try to help you. Many veterinarians can quickly gain access to literature and medications which are helpful for reptiles, and their efforts may save your iguana's life.

REFERENCES AND
RECOMMENDED READINGS

Anderson, N. L. 1991. Diseases of *Iguana iguana*. Compendium Contin. Educ. Pract. Vet. 14:1335- 1343.

Barten, S. L. 1993. The medical care of iguanas and other common pet lizards. *The Veterinary Clinics of North America Exotic Pet Medicine* I. Vol. 23: 6: 1213 - 1249.

Boyer, T. H. 1991. Common problems and treatment of the green iguana, *Iguana iguana. Bulletin of the Association of Reptilian and Amphibian Veterinarians* 1: 8 - 11.

_____. 1991. Green iguana care, *Bulletin of the Association of Reptilian and Amphibian Veterinarians* 1:12- 14.

de Vosjoli, Philippe. 1992. *The Green Iguana Manual.* Advanced Vivarium Systems Inc. Santee, Ca.

Donoghue, Susan. 1995. Nutrition Support. *Proceeding of the Association of Reptilian and Amphibian Veterinarians.* pp. 43 -49.

Frank, N. 1992. Green Iguanas: their care and captive husbandry. *Reptile and Amphibian Magazine.* Jan-Feb. pp. 30 -32.

Frye, Fredric. 1991. *Biomedical and Surgical Aspects of Captive Reptile Husbandry.* Vols. I and II. Krieger Publishing Co. Melbourne, Fl. 637 pp.

_____. 1995. *Iguana Iguana.* Krieger Publishing Co. Melbourne, Fl. 178 pp.

_____., D. R. Mader, B. V Centofanti. 1991. Interspecific (Lizard:human) aggression in captive iguanas (*Iguana iguana*). A preliminary compilation of eighteen cases. *Bulletin of Association of Reptilian and Amphibian Veterinarians.* 1:4 - 6, 1991.

Hatfield, J. 1996. *Green Iguana, The Ultimate Owner's Manual.* Dunthorpe Press. Portland, Oregon. 655 pp.

Nalverson, J. and D. Mader. 1995. DNA testing for sex identification in the green iguana (*Iguana iguana*). *Proceedings of the Association of Reptilian and Amphibian Veterinarians.* pp. 80.

Mader, D. R. (Ed.). 1996. *Reptile Medicine and Surgery.* Saunders Publishing Co. Philadelphia. 512 pp.

Rossi, John. 1994. The use of Soft Paws~in the Green Iguana. *Bulletin of the Association of Reptilian and Amphibian Veterinarians* 4 (1): 4.